Bad Boys of the New Testament
Exploring Men of
Questionable Virtue

BAD BOYS OF THE NEW TESTAMENT

EXPLORING MEN OF QUESTIONABLE VIRTUE

BARBARA J. ESSEX

The Pilgrim Press

Cleveland

DEDICATION

To Patricia, Christine, Gregory, Nathan,
and to the memory of Eddie.
You provide a circle of love and challenge that
makes me strong—thank you!

The Pilgrim Press, 700 Prospect Avenue, Cleveland, Ohio 44115-1100
thepilgrimpress.com

Printed in the United States of America on acid-free paper.

10 09 08 07 06 05   5 4 3 2 1

Library of Congress Cataloging-in-Publication Data

Essex, Barbara J. (Barbara Jean), 1951–
    Bad boys of the New Testament : exploring men of questionable virtue /
Barbara J. Essex.
        p.   cm.
    Includes bibliographical references (p.).
    ISBN 0-8298-1672-0 (paper. : alk. paper)
    1. Men in the Bible—Biography.   2. Bible. N.T.—Biography.   3. Bible.
N. T.—Criticism, interpretation, etc.   I. Title.

BS2430.E87   2005
225.9'22'081—dc22

2005043119

Contents

ACKNOWLEDGMENTS

I have gotten by—with a lot of help from my family and friends. I continue to thank God for those who push me to write: Kim Martin Sadler, Michael Lawrence, and their colleagues at The Pilgrim Press.

I am grateful for my conversation partners who have been extraordinarily patient and unrelentingly supportive during the writing of this volume—Ronald Williams-Wells, Patricia Essex, Edward Goode, Garfield Byrd, Ta-Tanisha Essex-Robinson, Linda Sroufe, Sheri Bryant, E. Ann Jefferson, Carolyn Young, and Opal Easter. Your support means more than I have words to express.

I appreciate the patience and challenge of my students at Catholic Theological Union (Chicago), Summer Institute 2003—thank you for pushing me to greater clarity and creativity as we wrestled with these "bad boys."

A special thanks to the folks at Pacific School of Religion who pushed and pushed and pushed until I got serious about finishing this book; your constant inquiries, "Are you finished with that book yet?" spurred me on—thank you, Chidinma, Archie, MDT, Faye, Terry, Tiffany, Marjorie, Diane, and Jane.

I owe a lifetime of gratitude to my mentors and teachers who opened the depths of the Bible and made it real for me: Jeremiah A. Wright, Jr., Carl H. Marbury, S. Dean McBride, George Polk, and Thomas Hoyt, Jr.

And, any strength of this volume is due to input from all who challenged and critiqued my thinking and research. All weaknesses are due to my own inadequacies.

GETTING STARTED

This Bible study is designed as a seven-week program for individual and/or group study. Leaders do not need extensive small group training. Each study unit reviews the stories of selected biblical men. A short commentary follows which provides background information to help make the story understandable for modern readers. Each unit ends with reflection questions to help start a discussion about what we can learn from these characters and their stories. This book is designed to help us examine our own motives, assumptions, and identity as we explore the stories of our faith.

The length of time for each session is one and a half to two hours; feel free, however, to make adjustments that work for you or your group. The materials you need include this book, a Bible version with which you are comfortable, and notebook or journal in which to record your answers and reflections.

A suggested format is:

➤ Assign readings ahead of time—the scripture as well as the unit to be studied.

➤ If necessary, set some "ground rules" for the discussion (for example, everyone will have an opportunity to voice his/her opinion without judgment from other group members; no one needs to agree with everyone else; no name calling; etc.)

➤ Begin each session with a prayer for open minds and meaningful discussion.

➤ Review the information in the study unit; answer any questions.

➤ Use the reflection questions at the end of each unit to start the discussion.

➤ Share insights about the text and as much as people feel comfortable with sharing.

➤ Assign the next unit.

➤ Close with prayer.

If you are using this resource for personal study, you should allot one and a half to two hours for each study unit. You will need a journal in which to record your reflections and questions.

At the end of this book, you will find a section with suggestions for preaching and teaching about these "bad boys." The bibliography and resources section lists additional books, articles, and websites that you may find helpful as you continue your studies. Of course, you should include any resources you find helpful to supplement the lessons here.

I encourage you to have fun; there is much to learn about these biblical folks as well as about ourselves. I hope that these study units will help deepen your faith and broaden your service towards others. I hope you find this study to be informative, challenging, and inspirational. Enjoy your journey.

More bad boys of the Bible? Of course! We wouldn't want to let the men of the New Testament off the hook, would we? There are a number of dubious characters in the New Testament that we want to examine more closely. What can we know about the Elder Brother of the Prodigal Son parable? What can we learn from the leadership decisions of Pilate? What really motivated the men who accuse the unnamed woman of adultery? Who are the "Pharisees" who are shamelessly blamed for Jesus' crucifixion? What was Judas thinking when he betrayed Jesus? These are burning questions that many of us dare not ask for fear of appearing less than faithful. Yet these often-unasked questions constitute the drama that makes the New Testament so powerful and so foundational to an understanding of our faith.

While I call the men in this book "bad boys," we know that they are a blend of both positive and negative qualities. In other words, they exhibit human characteristics and we can learn from them. We will attempt to discover whether they are historic figures or if they are metaphors to help us understand some aspect of life and faith. In our preaching and teaching, we sometimes overlook their flaws and sins, excuse their actions or downplay them. Their outrageous acts are seen as means to ends that support God's purpose and intentions. Some seemed destined to move the Gospel story along—are they captains of their destiny or mere pawns in God's plan of salvation? A closer look reveals very human, and sometimes, very base instincts and character flaws in these men, and sometimes, we see ourselves in their stories. Rather than wallow in guilt or preach damnation, I hope that we can acknowledge those less than lovely aspects of our own personalities mirrored in the stories of the "bad boys" and work to improve them. I hope, also, that we are moved to greater compassion and greater service on behalf of humanity. Finally, I hope we are reminded that God's grace and mercy are abundant and available to each of us as we make decisions and choices. The stories of the New Testament bad boys lay open to us a big picture of humankind and God's undying love for us.

I begin with the understanding that we will not study *all* the men in the New Testament. Exploring the characters of the disciples and the Apostle Paul would require many volumes—and some of this work has been done already. Of the six men I have selected, four of them (Judas, Pilate, the Pharisees, and the Accusers of the woman caught in adultery) have a direct relationship with Jesus; one of them (the Elder Brother of the Prodigal Son parable) is "invented" by Jesus; and one, Ananias, is a character of the early Christian Church. I have chosen these particular characters because they generate much controversy in our understanding of the faith and because they are familiar to us. Some of our assumptions will be called into question in this study. *Bad Boys of the New Testament* seeks to present a more informed, critical picture of biblical characters. I draw upon scholarship from feminist, Womanist, and other critical methods of reading and interpreting biblical texts.

It is assumed that you have little or no prior knowledge of the technical aspects of biblical exegesis. The next chapter serves as an overview of biblical methods of interpretation that will help you understand the background and context of the particular stories we will study. Some of the units will present us with challenges—we might be reluctant to analyze closely the biblical men for fear that we will offend God. We might be confronted with information that seems blasphemous. We might be tempted to reject the possible lessons available to us. We might simply refuse to believe what is written—but I encourage you to hang in there during the process! Critical study should not undermine your faith; instead, it should deepen, broaden, and expand it as you learn more about who these characters are and what motivates them. We are blessed to have sacred texts that give us pictures of real people who are not one-dimensional. We see the good, the bad, and the ugly—the Bible does not present perfect people. We are given the opportunity to see ourselves reflected in the stories of the persons we hold up as models of faith and service.

1

Overview of the New Testament and Biblical Study Methods

The Bible, the world's bestseller, is a book of words—words chosen by human beings who are shaped and influenced by the culture within which they live and work. Words change over time and are shaped by events of each era. The Bible was not originally written in English. The Hebrew Bible, also known as the Christian Old Testament, was written in Hebrew (except for parts of Daniel, Ezra, and one verse in Jeremiah written in Aramaic). The New Testament, also known as the Christian Scripture, was written in Greek. When we read the Bible, we are reading materials that have been translated into English. You are encouraged to use the version of the Bible with which you feel most comfortable. I will be using the New Revised Standard Version (NRSV) of the Bible. I will highlight Greek words when doing so helps us understand the text.

The New Testament is a continuation of a story that started in the Hebrew Bible. The term "New Testament" stems from an understanding that God has done something extraordinary in the person, ministry, death, and resurrection of Jesus. The writings of God's dealings with Israel are divided into old and new covenants, although there is no clean break in God's relationship with God's people. The terms, Old and New Testaments, became an easy way of designating the essence of God's dealings—the days of Moses and the prophets mark God's covenantal relationship with Israel; Jesus and Paul mark God's continual dealings with "Israel," a group now expanded to include diverse people. Rather than imply that the "New Testament" supercedes the "Old Testament," scholars designate the scriptures differently: Hebrew Bible and Christian Scripture. In order to understand the Christian faith, we must know our Jewish roots; therefore, the Bible is rightly inclusive of that which has gone before. Both "Testaments" serve as a witness to God's dealings with a particular group of people over a period of time. The central figure of the New Testament is Jesus of Nazareth. His life, ministry, death, and resurrection form the core of Christianity.

Just as God acted in history for the Israelites, God continues to act to bring people into God's realm. God liberated God's people from bondage in Egypt and brought them into community with God and with each other. God continues reaching out—this time through the death and resurrection of Jesus of Nazareth who showed the world how to live as children of God.

Despite wide diversity in the expression of this faith tradition, belief in Jesus as the Son of God is essential. The writer of the letter to the Ephesians makes this clear:

> *I therefore, the prisoner in the Lord, beg you to lead a life worthy of the calling to which you have been called, with all humility and gentleness, with patience, bearing with one another in love, making every effort to maintain the unity of the Spirit in the bond of peace. There is one body and one Spirit, just as you were called to the one hope of your calling, one Lord, one faith, one baptism, one God and Father of all, who is above all and through all and in all.*
> (EPHESIANS 4:1–6)

God's work through Jesus has given birth to what is now a major player on the world stage of religions. There are millions of Christians around the world who express their faith in a variety of ways and all revolve around the central figure of the New Testament.

There are twenty-seven books in the New Testament with at least four literary forms:

> ➤ The Gospels are the first four books of the New Testament. "Gospel" means "good news" and they tell of Jesus' birth, baptism, ministry of word and service, death, and resurrection. The four Gospels are

Matthew, Mark, Luke, and John. Each has a particular perspective on the Christ event.

➤ A book of history, the Acts of the Apostles, tells of the birth and growth of Christianity during the first thirty years or so after Jesus' death and resurrection.

➤ A section of twenty-one letters to individuals and church communities addresses various issues of the early church.

➤ A final book, Revelation, is an apocalyptic book that deals with God's will for the future.

We have no existing words written by Jesus himself. His followers wrote what we know about him and his disciples based on oral traditions. Scholars generally agree that the earliest written account of Jesus is that of Mark's Gospel. Tradition has it that Mark was a disciple of Peter. Mark's account, supplemented by other traditions, is the foundation for the Gospels by Matthew and Luke. These three Gospels are so much alike that they are called "synoptic." They highlight the public ministry of Jesus in Galilee.

On the other hand, the Gospel of John, the Fourth Gospel, highlights Jesus' ministry in Judea. It is so different from the others that it is designated as "asynoptic."

The letters of the New Testament were written by a number of teachers to instruct and inspire the early church. In any new movement, there are bound to be issues and problems that require attention. The epistle, or letter, is the perfect form to teach and reprimand as well as to lift up the tenets of the faith. The letters, then, often deal with weighty issues and maintain a note of intimacy and care.

A concern that confuses modern readers of the Bible has to do with the sequencing of the letters. The letters are not arranged chronologically but rather, according to length. The longer letters are placed first. Thus, there are places where it is difficult to understand what is happening.

The Hebrew Bible (Old Testament) is written in Hebrew and Aramaic; the New Testament is written in Greek. Those languages are more adept at nuance than English translations, and we must work harder to understand what the Bible means and intends. There are a number of ways of getting behind the stories we find in the New Testament. A brief survey of methods includes:

> ➤ Literary Criticism looks at the contexts, plots, and character development in the stories;

> ➤ Rhetorical Criticism determines the types of stories and their purposes; some stories are not "personal" but are stylized ways of talking about others—we believe such is the case with much that is said about Jesus' opponents in the New Testament (especially the Pharisees and "Jews");

> ➤ Historical Criticism tries to get behind the story to see which circumstances gave rise to the stories and how circumstances were understood by the communities out of which the stories came;

> ➤ Reader-Response Criticism deals with how characters in the stories hear and react to the action as well as how we hear and react to them today;

> ➤ Redaction Criticism outlines the interaction and connection between a tradition and a later interpretative point of view; that is, the concern is with how smaller units from oral tradition or written sources were put together to form larger passages. Also, redaction criticism uncovers the writer's theological motivation by asking: for whom was the tradition written, for what reasons was it written and what situation gave rise to the tradition.

The important task for serious students of the Bible is to ask the following questions:

1. What is the story about? What is the story?

2. Who "wrote" this book? What is the theological agenda of the writer?

3. What divine purposes does the story serve?

4. Who gains by the telling of the story? What is gained?

5. What is the historical, political, social, and theological background for this passage?

6. What are the lessons of this story for us today?

In the area of Source Criticism, it is widely agreed that the Gospel of Mark provides the basic outline for the Synoptic Gospels; Mark is the source of information for Matthew and Luke. However, Matthew and Luke share material not found in Mark and each has material unique to itself. These sources are unrecoverable and are designated as: "M" for Matthew's extra material; "L" for Luke's extra material; and "Q" for material that Matthew and Luke share that is not in Mark. "Q" is believed to be a collection of sayings of Jesus. It is believed that these materials are bits of oral and written traditions that were in circulation shortly after the resurrection but prior to the writing of the Gospels.

Each Gospel has a unique perspective on the Christ event and grows out of concerns dominant in those communities that produced them. Each of the Synoptic Gospels has a year designated for it in the lectionary (Matthew–Year A; Mark–Year B; Luke–Year C); but John does not! But parts of John are used at important points in the Christian year—Christmas, Lent, and Easter. A brief overview follows:

> Matthew connects the Gospel story with God's saving acts in the Hebrew Bible (Matthew opens with a lengthy genealogy that links Jesus back to Abraham). Matthew wants to show that Jesus is God's fulfillment promised in the law and the prophets and that the church is a continuation of God's ongoing work of redemption. Yet Matthew is the only Gospel that speaks of the "church" as the community of believers. Matthew speaks to a Jewish Christian audience as well as to Gentiles. As the leading religious leaders, the Pharisees saw their

responsibility as that of keeping the faith and downplaying the
Christian movement. Matthew's community was deeply involved in
trying to show how Jesus is God's Messiah, long anticipated by the
children of Israel. Matthew sees his community in a waiting period
where they must be missionaries (see Matt. 28:19–20) until Jesus
returns to claim his church. The Gospel is dated late first century,
perhaps 90 CE.

➤ Mark's is the earliest written account of the Jesus story. He intends
for his work to be a "gospel" (see Mark 1:1). Jesus is the "Son of
God" and the cross is key to understanding Jesus' identity and his
purposes. Mark's audience is primarily Gentile; his community's
suffering at the hands of the Roman government and the Jewish
leaders of the synagogue mirrors the suffering of Jesus during his
passion. Mark's agenda reflects a more historical than a biographical
concern. God has intervened, once again, in history to redeem the
time and to redeem God's people. The date of the Gospel is around
65–70 CE.

➤ Luke presumes to write a more objective story about Jesus and his
works—read Luke 1:1–4. This Gospel is more "historical" than the
others in that Luke includes the names and dates of persons found in
works outside the Bible. Luke also includes information about the
early church in his work (the Gospel and the Book of Acts). Jesus is
the Messiah who ushers in God's new world order that is radically
inclusive–Luke talks a great deal about outcasts, women, and sinners
who are included in Jesus' sphere of forgiveness and fellowship. The
date is difficult to pinpoint, somewhere around 70–90 CE, probably
mid-80s.

➤ John continues to generate a great deal of scholarly debate about
authorship and date. About the most we can say with certainty is that
a Jewish Christian whose community had been cast out of the synagogue composed the Gospel. John's Gospel is different enough from
Matthew, Mark and Luke to be labeled asynoptic. John's book is
filled with different images and symbols as it tells the story of Jesus.

Instead of short moral teachings and instructions that we find in the Synoptics, John shows Jesus speaking in long discourses and having long debates with his opponents. Most of the discourses and debates show the validity of Jesus' messiahship and relationship to God. Jesus' words serve to confuse people, even his disciples, and Jesus is often misunderstood. There are many references to Hebrew Scripture and John uses dualities to express the meaning of the Jesus event. John's mission is to persuade people that Jesus is God's Chosen One and God's fulfillment to bring eternal life to the world. A likely date for the Gospel is 100 CE.

The New Testament world was much different from ours today. People in the time of Jesus had their own cultural norms and patterns. The society was agriculturally based with a number of social groups or classes. Farming technology allowed the people to produce what was needed for the survival of the society and allowed surplus products. The surplus created a class of leisure that needed luxury goods and services. Thus, social classes developed based on who had money and those who did not: there were those who owned land, those who administered the various roles of government, those who worked the land, those who supervised the workers, those who produced luxury items and those chronically unemployed—those with mental and physical challenges, women, children, and "aliens" or outsiders. The priestly and religious leaders were a separate class and had ties to both the haves and have-nots. There were constant struggles as those of the "haves" tried to keep their power, status, and wealth; so, a military class was needed to keep law and order. Issues of justice and fair play would be prevalent for the "have-nots." Those in the middle simply tried to stay out of trouble as they tried to move up the ladder.

Conflict was handled in predictable ways. Trouble arose when one of the parties involved stepped outside the protocol. The conflicts in the New Testament focus primarily around issues of power/authority, gender status, and religion. The predominant framework for the shape of the stories we will explore is *patriarchy*. The underlying assumption for all of the traditions is the superiority of men. God-loving people in the early centuries of the church reaffirmed and maintained patriarchy in spite of Jesus' explicit affirmation of the worth and equality of all people—men, women, children, and outcasts! Patriarchy sets up the legal systems and makes official male dominance over women and children. It means that men hold the power and leadership in the important public and military institutions of society. Features of patriarchy include the understandings that: the family is the basic unit and is headed by a father; family history is traced through the father's blood lines; and women's roles are primarily those of wife and mother, especially mother of male children.

A man retains his honor as long as he: controls the behavior of others, especially family members (the father in the Prodigal Son parable is shamed by his son's departure and his honor is restored when the son returns; he is shamed again when the older son refuses to join the celebration of the younger son's return); maintains the boundaries between men and women where each knows their place (Jesus is "shameful" in his interactions with women whom he treats with respect and whom he values); maintains proper reverence for religious traditions (Jesus shames the Pharisees and other opponents because he breaks protocol; this angers them to no end). The honor-shame dichotomy is prevalent in the New Testament and forms the basis for much of the conflict between Jesus and religious leaders. The interplay is about challenge and response and jockeying for position—the sparring is humorous in some places, but eventually leads Jesus to the cross. The challenge and response move only happens between parties that are socially equal. The Pharisees, for example, deal with Jesus as their equal and feel threatened by him. The high priest and Pilate, on the other hand, do not see Jesus as their equal and therefore are less invested in what happens to Jesus.

There is much going on behind the scenes of the stories we will explore. We cannot simply take the stories or their characters at face value. We need to peer behind them to see what else may be happening in the action of the stories. This overview is, by necessity, brief and simplistic. But it will help us ask the right questions as we look at selected "bad boys."

Well, it's time to begin. Have a great time hanging out with these "bad boys" of the New Testament!

2

THE ELDER BROTHER: "IT'S NOT FAIR! WHERE IS MY PARTY?"

READ LUKE 15:11–32

The story of the Elder Brother of the Prodigal Son parable is that of a man who is envious of his brother and feels unappreciated by his father. He is inhospitable and hostile when his wayward brother returns home. He accuses his brother of all kinds of evils even though he does not know for sure what happened. He disrespects his father and refuses to join in the celebration of his brother's return.

Tsk! Tsk! Tsk! Poor Elder Brother. This story is about a son who behaves badly. Actually, it is a story about two sons behaving badly. Tension between brothers is nothing new in the Bible. Cain and Abel, Jacob and Esau, Joseph and his brothers all speak to troubled family relationships and the effects of sibling rivalry. All of these cases highlight the feelings of older brothers who are displaced by the younger brother:

- In Gen. 4:1–16, God rejects Cain and his offering. Cain kills his brother, Abel, and shows little or no remorse;

- In Gen. 27:1–40, Jacob steals his brother's birthright and tricks his father, Isaac, into giving him the blessing due the elder son. Jacob's purpose is to claim the seat and rights of the elder son, Esau.

- In Gen. chapters 39–50, Joseph is the favored son of Jacob. Joseph is sold into slavery by his jealous brothers and given up for dead. In the end, Joseph is the one who saves his family from starvation (Gen. 50:15–21).

The Bible constantly passes over older brothers and elevates the younger sibling. And now we are faced with two brothers in this parable. The issue of sibling rivalry is not dead yet. However, our primary focus here is on the Elder Brother.

The Elder Brother's story is embedded in what is commonly known as the Parable of the Prodigal Son. It is a well-known story and many sermons and church school lessons have been based on this parable. Sermons and lessons most often highlight several aspects of the parable: (a) some of us need to hit rock bottom before we can truly become who we are meant to be; (b) God is like the patient father waiting to receive us into God's household; (c) too many of us are like the pouting Elder Brother resentful of those whom God embraces. Most of our preaching and teaching has a focus on love, repentance, and forgiveness. And the Elder Brother symbolizes the worst example of very human attitudes and feelings. Those of us who, at times, may harbor resentment and jealousy are made to feel unworthy of God's blessings. I want to suggest that Jesus is saying something much more profound about God's Realm here. Further, I suggest that the Elder Brother is justified in feeling the way he does; but what he does with those feelings will ultimately determine the kind of person he is.

A first task is to have some understanding of the parable by defining just what a parable is. The Greek, *parabole*, denotes a comparison. A general understanding of parables is based in the saying, "As in heaven, so on earth." That is, the parable is an earthly story with a heavenly meaning. Parables are generally rooted in something familiar to the hearers, such as some aspect of nature or everyday life. The parable then makes a connection to some spiritual truth or expectation that illustrates the character or action of God or God's Realm. The parables of Jesus deal with God's Realm (Kingdom) and/or the future state of humanity. Further, the parables of Jesus demand a response from the hearers and, by extension, from us. Scholars are questioning this simplistic view of the parable. In fact, scholars, including William R. Herzog II, suggest that the parables are not just simple stories about

being faithful but rather are scathing indictments on the power struc-
tures of Jesus' day. In his book, *Parables as Subversive Speech: Jesus as
Pedagogue of the Oppressed*, Herzog outlines the agrarian society of Jesus'
day and gives us a picture that mirrors our modern United States. The
advanced agrarian society was stratified into the "haves" and the "have-
nots." Those in power, who formed a small minority, controlled the economic, political, and social spheres of existence. At their disposal was
military power to reinforce their efforts to maintain and expand their
wealth. The vast majority of people were barely eking out a living and
were at the mercy of those in power. They were heavily taxed. Many of
them were not able to keep up with their tax payments.

Taxes fell into three primary categories: direct taxes, indirect taxes
or tolls, and Temple taxes. Agents employed by the Roman government collected direct taxes, including poll taxes and land taxes. These
agents were known as tax collectors and had the military force of the
Empire to protect their collection efforts. The people seemed to
accept this taxation obligation as a given in their life as subjects to the
Roman Empire.

In contrast to the tax collectors was a group known as "toll collectors." It was the toll collector who appears in the Gospels and has been
misidentified as tax collector. Toll collectors were responsible for indirect taxes, including tolls, tariffs, custom fees and such collected at
tollhouses. Toll collectors generally worked for chief toll collectors
who bought the right by a contract agreement to collect the money.
The chief toll collector paid the fees due up front and had to recoup
his investment at the tollbooths. The chief toll collector had to raise
the tolls high enough to cover his investment and to make a profit. The
object was not to collect fees that would benefit the common good; it
was to make more money for the chief toll collectors. This paved the
way for fraud and exploitation. Since toll collectors barely earned
enough to sustain themselves, they were notorious for hiking up
prices even more and skimming off the top before turning the money
over to their employers. The toll collectors were seen as "outsiders"
because they were used by the oppressive ruling and elite class to

exploit poor people. These men were considered lower than low because they were pawns doing their masters' bidding with no regard for the people from whom they collected tolls.

A third area of taxation is related to the Temple. The priests collected the Temple tax for the upkeep of the religious institution. The priests, working for the rich elite, provided the rationale for the order of society. Their ideology encouraged the masses of people to pay their taxes and to be good citizens. Failure to comply resulted in persons being castigated by the religious authorities. The religious authorities gave legitimacy to the economic, political and social order that benefited the haves to the detriment of the have-nots. Why did they do this? In a society where land, power and money ruled, even those who should have known better succumbed to the temptation. The priests tried to accumulate land and have their land exempt from taxes. This worked to their advantage most of the time. If a priest was denied exemption from taxes, he had the option of becoming a "prophetic presence" in opposition to the government. It is suggested that great efforts were made to keep the peace and ward off insurrections and coup attempts. In Jesus' day, the keepers of the faith were the Pharisees. Their judgment resulted in persons being labeled "unclean" which carried social implications.

While the tax collector had the benefit of the government and the military to protect his interest, there was no such sanction available to the toll collectors. The people despised the toll collectors because there was no protection against their exploitation. The actions of the toll collectors were seen as acts of injustice and exploitation. They were beyond redemption according to the religious authorities; redemption would mean making restitution plus paying interest to those exploited. Because the toll collector dealt with an ever-changing population, there was no reasonable way he could make restitution. While direct and indirect taxes were mandatory, Temple taxes were not. Yet, failure to pay the Temple assessment plunged one into a spiritual morass—nonpayment was the basis for being ostracized and cast out of the circle of faith.

This context is important if we are to glean some lessons from the Parable of the Prodigal Son. On the surface, the parable seems self-explanatory. It is the third parable in Luke 15 that Jesus utters concerning finding that which has been lost and celebrating the recovery of the lost. The first parable is about a lost sheep (see Luke 15:3–7) and the second is about a lost coin (see Luke 15:8–10). Both parables share the same structure: each begins with a question; each relates a loss; the lost is found; the seeker invites friends to rejoice and celebrate the recovery; and each ends with a statement about the joy in heaven or among angels at the recovery of the lost. In each of the two parables, the one who seeks what is lost works hard to recover the loss.

All three parables in Luke 15 are set in the context of an encounter between Jesus and the so-called Pharisees and scribes—read Luke 15:1–2. Jesus and the Pharisees are at odds about Jesus' tendency to welcome the outsider—women, toll collectors, foreigners and sinners. Jesus' interactions with these outsiders are a source of consternation with the Pharisees and their cohorts. The Pharisees are quick to express their dissatisfaction with Jesus' choice of disciples and table companions. In the context of Luke and this parable, the toll collectors were the lowest of the low for the reasons outlined above. It is in this context that an important lesson of the parable emerges.

Luke 15 begins with a line drawn in the sand:

> *Now all the tax collectors and sinners were coming near to listen to him. And the Pharisees and the scribes were grumbling and saying, "This fellow welcomes sinners and eats with them." So he told them this parable . . . "*(LUKE 15:1–3A)

Jesus hangs out with toll collectors and even invited one to join him in his mission. Further, he dines with them and enjoys himself! (Read Luke 5:27–32; 14:1; and 19:1–10). Then Jesus tells the three parables we have in Luke 15. The moral of the first two parables revolves around finding a lost object. Sinners, represented by the lost sheep and lost coin, are found and their recovery is celebrated. Certainly such a scenario in heaven and among angels would make the scribes and Pharisees bristle with self-righteous indignation. They had great problems with heaven being peopled by what they considered to be the dredges of society. But Jesus doesn't stop there—he digs the knife even deeper into their psyches.

The Parable of the Prodigal Son is actually a story about a man and his two sons. The younger son defies convention and asks for his inheritance before the father dies. His request is unusual but the father complies without comment or argument. He divided his property between the two sons. The Greek word translated as "property" is *bios*, which means "life." The Greek *bios* is about the length of life and the means of supporting that life. The father breaks his life to honor the request of his son. A part of the father dies when the son leaves. The family is disrupted, the circle is broken; the father is somehow incomplete without his son. The father gives up part of his life, his *bios*, to the younger son.

Shortly after receiving his share of the father's property, the younger son leaves and travels to a distant land where he squanders his inheritance. The Greek word, *asotos*, is translated here as "dissolute living" ("wild living" in the NIV). The same word occurs only three other times in the New Testament and the meaning refers to indulging in vices and a lack of moral discipline (see Ephesians 5:18; Titus 1:6; and 1 Peter 4:3). The text does not spell out the young man's activities in detail but he may have indulged in drunkenness, licentiousness, carousing, and total rebelliousness.

He ends up feeding pigs, an activity denounced by Jewish tradition. His downward spiral is complete when he considers eating the carob pods he is feeding to the swine. He is living the consequences of his decision to leave home—he has spent everything; he is starving; he is in a pigpen—and no one gives him anything (Luke 15:14–16).

He has a conversation with himself and decides to go back home. His thought is to hire himself as a servant in his father's household since he has already given up his status as son. His father owes him nothing since the son has already claimed his inheritance. He humbles himself, rehearses his speech, and heads home (Luke 15:17–19). What's the worst that can happen?

As he approaches home, he can't believe his eyes. Running toward him is his father who puts his arms around his son and kisses him (the scene reminds us of Jacob and Esau's reunion in Gen. 33:4). Before the son can finish his speech, the father interrupts him, see Luke 15:20–21.

The father would have been within his rights to chastise the son and send him away. He could have cursed him and kept him out of the circle. He could have ordered his servants to escort the son off of his property–for he was trespassing and uninvited.

But the father surprises his son and surprises us. He orders his servants to bring the best robe, a valued ring, and a pair of sandals. He welcomes his son back into the family and restores his status as son. No longer is the son estranged, no longer is he outside the family circle–he is, once again, son. He belongs to a family; he was lost, but is now found; was as good as dead but now alive and well (Luke 15:22–24). The son's return was cause for a grand celebration–good food, good music, good dancing, joy, laughter, and fun.

Up to this point, the Elder Brother has been silent. The action has been between the father and the younger son; about the son in a distant land; and between the father and younger son again. Their relationship has come full circle. That which was broken has been restored and all is right with the world . . . well, not quite.

We finally meet the Elder Brother in Luke 15:25—he appears after the homecoming celebration for the younger son has begun. The Elder Brother was so out of the loop that he asked one of the servants what was happening (Luke 15:26–27). When he hears the news, he is fit to be tied—he can't believe it! This boy has been gone all this time (we don't know how long) and doing only God knows what (but we have our suspicions) and he suddenly shows up and Dad throws a party and slaughters the fatted calf! How could he!

The Elder Brother refuses to go in to join the celebration. The father comes out of the house to meet the son—just as he went out to meet the returning Prodigal. Even more, the father pleads with his Elder Son to come in and join the party (Luke 15:28).

To his credit, the Elder Brother states his case:

But he answered his father, 'Listen! For all these years I have been working like a slave for you, and I have never disobeyed your command; yet you have never given me even a young goat so that I might celebrate with my friends. But when this son of yours came back, who has devoured your property with prostitutes, you killed the fatted calf for him!'(LUKE 15:29–30)

Do you think the Elder Brother has an issue with his brother's return? The text does not tell us the source of the brother's anger and resentment, but we can make some guesses.

No doubt the Elder Brother is resentful of his younger sibling. He didn't have the privilege of getting his inheritance early and getting out of town. As the elder son, he is entitled to a double portion of his father's estate. But he chose to honor tradition and wait until his father's retirement or death in order to claim what is due him. He stays behind to take care of the family; no mention is made of his mother, whether he has other siblings, or if he is married with children.

The Elder Brother fulfills his obligations and is clearly resentful about his choice. Notice that the brothers never interact with one another; they only interact with their father. The younger brother never refers to his big brother at all. The Elder Brother never claims his younger sibling as brother—he is his father's son *(This son of yours . . .).*

Sibling rivalry is a theme that runs throughout the Bible. We are accustomed to the animosity and hostility between siblings, which result in all manner of behavior:

➤ Cain murders his brother;

➤ Jacob and Esau eventually reconcile but only after Esau's murderous plot is exposed and Jacob is sent away to preserve his life;

➤ Joseph's brothers throw him in a pit and sell him into slavery but they are eventually rescued by Joseph;

➤ Rachel and Leah find a way to peacefully coexist although they are married to and bear children for the same man.

Sibling rivalry is rooted in a competition for a perceived scarcity: attention, love, affection, or parental approval. The "winner" has exclusive use or control of the commodity at stake; the "loser" feels deprived. Both want to feel needed, loved, and attended to; the parents must work to find a balance so that no child feels left out or neglected. If parents don't strike that balance, one child or another reacts emotionally and lodges his or her frustration upon the other sibling. This antagonism for the younger sibling too often develops before the elder child has the capacity to process his or her thoughts in a rational, logical, or conscious manner.

Without thinking about it, the elder child may act out to get the parent to stop loving the younger child. The action of the older child is to gain back the parents' undivided attention. The elder also might aggravate or bother the younger child directly. In classic cases of sibling rivalry, there is a tug of war with the children—the elder trying to gain the upper hand and control over the younger, and the younger trying to defend him/herself against the barbs of the older sibling.

In many cases, the competition does not result in violence; but parents should be aware of what is happening with their children. In our parable, the father seeks to satisfy both his sons. He does not argue when the younger son wants to leave him. The father indulges the son's wanderlust and sends him on his way. We presume the father wishes his son well as he takes his leave from the family. We know that the father is elated when the son returns. The father does not require an explanation or even an apology. He welcomes his son back with open arms and unconditional love.

When the Elder Brother vents his anger and resentment, the father does not blame him. The father listens to and acknowledges the son's feelings. In some ways, the Elder Brother can't help feeling the way he does. His problem with his brother is a universal and timeless one. The Elder Brother has stayed at home and has done the right thing for all the right reasons. But where is his party? How does he know that he is loved and appreciated and cherished? Where is his reward for doing what he is supposed to do?

As Thomas L. Hoyt, Jr. points out, the Elder Brother fails to see the big picture. The celebration is not a reward for the younger son's abandonment of the family; the celebration is about his re-embracing the family. The younger brother did squander his resources and he may have had a good time doing so (notice the Elder Brother accuses him of cavorting with harlots—perhaps projecting his own desires?). But the bottom line is that the family is incomplete without him. His return restores the family and that is the reason for the celebration.

As the firstborn, the Elder Brother is probably serious, conscientious, rule conscious, responsible, and demanding. These are traits that psychologists assign to firstborns. They seek their parents' approval and learn early on how to get it. Firstborns are generally high achievers and strive to live up to their parents' expectations. At the same time, firstborns are anxious about maintaining their place in their parents' lives. To fail would be nearly devastating. Firstborns work harder to excel and set very high standards for themselves—which means that they rarely relax or feel satisfied with the status quo.

The father tries to assure the elder son that he is loved equally and unconditionally. The Elder Brother is always within the household, always with the father, has never been lost or dead. He takes for granted his ongoing privilege of inclusion. He sees the return of the Prodigal as an attempt to displace him rather than as a return to wholeness and harmony in the household. The father is tender with his son and tries to help him see the bigger picture:

> Then the father said to him, 'Son, you are always with me, and all that is mine is yours. But we had to celebrate and rejoice, because this brother of yours was dead and has come to life; he was lost and has been found.'"
> LUKE 15:31–32

The Elder Brother is justified in feeling the way he does. It's not his fault he was born first. It's not a liability to be responsible and dependable. His feelings of anger, jealousy, and resentment are natural feelings. He has not allowed himself to be adventurous nor has he indulged in things that bring him pleasure. He's been so busy working for and with his father that he hardly knows what fun is.

We cannot blame the Elder Brother for how he feels. We can learn, however, something about his character by how he responds to his father's words in verses 31–32.

There are a number of ways to interpret the meaning of this parable. Let's look at a couple of models in broad strokes. Mary A. Tolbert proposes a model based on Freudian psychology. Using Sigmund Freud's theory, she outlines how the characters of the parable represent aspects of our personalities:

➤ The Id is that aspect that allows us to have our basic needs met; the id wants that which feels good without thinking about reality or consequences. The younger son symbolizes the id.

➤ The Ego is based in reality; the ego tries to satisfy the id with an understanding of boundaries and limitation. The Elder Brother represents the ego.

➤ The Superego is the moral aspect of our personalities; the superego is equated with the conscience that determines our sense of right and wrong. The father represents the super ego.

Tolbert's premise is that the parable is about the restoration of unity and about reconciliation. She sees the inside / outside dichotomy as the focus of the parable. Being in the house represents balance and harmony while being out of the house represents conflict. The parable, then, is about the father's attempt to integrate the family and bring about wholeness by having both sons back in the house. Her theory has merit in that the father's actions related to bringing both sons back into the family. The younger son, having lived a life of unrestrained pleasure, is welcomed home—both he and his father want him home. The younger son is able to recognize his alienation from the family and seeks to rejoin the circle even though he recognizes that his status has changed (he was as good as dead). But the father yearns for him and restores his status as son and the family is whole again. While the younger son chooses to be on the outside initially, the father has taken him back in and, ultimately, the son chooses to be inside.

The Elder Brother has always been on the inside but did not recognize or appreciate his status. Upon the return of the younger son, we see that the Elder Brother is alienated from the family, too. The father goes out and pleads with the Elder Brother to come into the house—to be joined to the family so that wholeness prevails. The Elder Brother has a decision to make—the offer to complete the circle and restore the family to wholeness has been extended. The parable ends without telling us what the Elder Brother does. What will we do with the offer that is extended to us? Will we stay stuck in our resentment, jealousy, and anger or will we go inside, join the celebration, and live in wholeness?

In a similar way, Dan O. Via, Jr. uses a Jungian model to interpret the parable. Via, too, believes that the parable's theme is about integration but uses Jungian categories:

➤ The Self is concerned with wholeness; it is the totality and center, which the father personifies in the parable.

➤ The Shadow consists of those aspects that have been repressed and symbolizes the inferior parts of our being. The Elder Brother symbolizes our Shadow side.

➤ The Ego represents the role we choose to live, the center of our consciousness, which the younger brother symbolizes.

Again, Via's perspective leads to wholeness—the function of the parable is to rejoin the ego to the self by coming to terms with the shadow.

Of course, both Tolbert and Via go into much more depth as they present their arguments. For our purposes, this very brief and somewhat simplistic summary is enough to lead us to some concluding words about the parable.

It is important to remember the context in which Jesus tells this parable. He is addressing the dissatisfaction of the scribes and Pharisees concerning his choice of companions. In answer to their grumbling in 15:2, Jesus tells stories about the radical inclusiveness of God's Realm (Kingdom). Jesus challenges their standard of entrance into God's household by saying that God reaches out to those shunned even by religious leaders—sinners, women, and even the lowly toll collectors.

Jesus lives out his understanding of God's intention and purposes by fellowshipping with unlikely folks. God includes the outsiders by actively seeking them—like lost sheep and lost coins. Further, God does not seek the outsider to the exclusion of those already on the inside (i.e., the Elder Brother). Rather, God seeks both sinner and saint into the divine household. And if the scribes and Pharisees take their faith seriously, they, too, will join in the celebration over the recovery of that which is lost.

We cannot judge who is in and who is out—that prerogative belongs solely to God. Thus, the modern church's squabbles over who is worthy to be included must be seen as antithetical to God's vision of humanity and creation and is a slap in the face given the nature and scope of Jesus' ministry.

Indeed, Jesus is so convinced of God's desire for wholeness that he puts his life on the line to live out God's purposes. Jesus spends a great deal of time interacting with the outsiders of his day. And he answered every challenge of the established religious authority. He did not back down or compromise his ministry to fit in. Instead, Jesus modeled a different way of being and his actions were both radical and subversive.

The Elder Brother in this parable represents all of us who feel displaced by God's embrace of those whom we reject. The father in the parable shows us that God wants both sinner and saint—not one over the other; not one in favor of the other. All people are to be given respect and dignity. Just like the Elder Brother, we have to make the decision to join the celebration or remain outside, feeling dejected and abandoned.

Discipleship requires us to be in relationship with others, not separated from them. We cannot put limits on God's goodness; there is enough love to go around.

REFLECTION QUESTIONS

1. Does the discussion about the political and social background of the parable change the way you see it? Explain.

2. Describe a time when you felt like you were on the outside looking in.

3. What makes you feel valued? Appreciated? Included? Diminished? Insecure? Worthy? Explain your answer.

4. What advice do you offer parents who must mediate sibling rivalry among their children?

5. In what ways do the family dynamics in the parable mirror or diverge from your own family of origin? Explain.

6. What role does trust play in family dynamics? In leadership development?

7. How do you deal with anger? Resentment? Envy? Are your methods healthy? Why or why not?

8. What could make the Elder Brother feel better about his choice to stay at home?

9. What role should the mother play in this parable?

10. What role should God play in family life?

3

ACCUSERS OF THE WOMAN CAUGHT IN ADULTERY: "NOWHERE TO RUN, NOWHERE TO HIDE"

READ JOHN 7:53–8:11

> *This is a familiar Bible story. A group of men have caught a woman in the act*
> *of adultery whom they bring before Jesus for judgment. The men are testing Jesus*
> *to determine where he stands in relationship to Mosaic law. Jesus, however, is not*
> *easily trapped and has a word for them and for the woman—and for us!*

The story commonly known as "The Woman Caught in Adultery" is only found in the Gospel of John. In this Gospel, Jesus engages in lengthy conversations about Mosaic law and its interpretation. Jesus is shown in conflict with the Jewish leaders of the day. The leaders are always "testing" Jesus—they want to bring a charge of blasphemy against him to squash his ministry.

In chapters seven and eight, John weaves parts of the Jesus tradition into a picture of intensifying conflict between Jesus and Jewish leaders in Jerusalem. The backdrop for 7:53–8:11 is the Feast of Booths (or Tabernacles), one of three major pilgrimage festivals of Judaism (the others are Passover and Festival of Weeks or Pentecost). The Festival of Booths was a joyous harvest celebration where people set up tents/booths and live in them for eight days in commemoration of God's protection during the wilderness wandering (see Lev. 23:39–43). In the eyes of his opponents, Jesus does not faithfully or rightly interpret the law of Moses. Jewish leaders set out to test Jesus by demanding that he "rightly" interpret the law. Jesus plays their game to their disadvantage. Ultimately, this episode is not about the sin of the woman or a just penalty, but is a story about a challenge to Jesus' honor, authority, and power by a group of scribes and

Pharisees. Jesus' unwillingness to "toe the line" thwarts the Jewish leaders' desire to undermine Jesus' ministry and mission.

There is some question among scholars about whether this passage, 7:53–8:11, is an original part of John's Gospel. The earliest manuscripts do not include it. In fact, the NRSV places the text in brackets to indicate its unresolved textual history. Scholars cite a number of reasons for questioning its Johannine origin. This passage is the only place in the Fourth Gospel where:

➤ The Mount of Olives is mentioned (8:1) although this is the site that Jesus visits often when near Jerusalem in the Synoptics;

➤ The "scribes" are referred to (8:3), although they appear frequently in the Synoptics;

➤ Jesus is referred to as "Teacher" (8:4) which is a title used often in the Synoptics.

These points, in addition to questions about style and language, lead scholars to the belief that this is a non-Johannine story that somehow found its way into the Fourth Gospel. Many commentators suggest that the story may not have belonged to John's Gospel but is a real incident in the ministry of Jesus.

The story begins with the scribes and Pharisees bringing an unnamed woman to the Temple while Jesus is teaching the crowd there. The men interrupt Jesus' lesson—they make the disheveled, half-dressed woman stand before Jesus. They say to Jesus:

> ..."Teacher, this woman was caught in the very act of committing adultery. Now in the law Moses commanded us to stone such women. Now what do you say?" They said this to test him, so that they might have some charge to bring against him. Jesus bent down and wrote with his finger on the ground. (JOHN 8:4–6)

The penalty for adultery, according to Mosaic law, is stoning to death. Two witnesses are needed for a conviction. According to the law, though, both adulterous parties are to be punished (see Dt. 22:22).

But the scribes and Pharisees are not really there to judge the woman—they are there to judge Jesus. If their concern were the actual act of adultery, they would have made sure their case was airtight by providing the necessary credible witnesses according to the law (see Dt. 19:15–21). In addition, in cases of adultery, both the man and the woman must be judged (see Lev. 20:10 and Dt. 22:22). The spirit of the law concerning adultery, in fact, has more to do with a man's honor than any concern for the woman. Women were seen as property and the law sought to protect men's property.

So the scribes and Pharisees make clear their intentions with Jesus—the law and the woman merely present an opportunity for them to test Jesus. Jesus, though, is keenly aware of their despicable attempt and he refuses to be entrapped. Instead of answering their question, Jesus ignores them, bends down and writes with his finger upon the ground. In ancient days, Jesus' action was clear non-acceptance of their challenge.

The scribes and Pharisees recognize Jesus' unwillingness to be challenged, but they continue to harass Jesus. Jesus rises and utters those oh so familiar words: *"Let anyone among you who is without sin be the first to throw a stone at her." (John 8:7b)*

If there is to be a debate or argument, Jesus will set the parameters. Jesus changes the debate by holding the scribes and Pharisees accountable to the very law they hold so dear. Jesus does not deny or question the Mosaic punishment—he tells them to throw the stones, *but only if they are innocent of sin themselves!*

Jesus has turned their trap back on them. If any of them throws a stone, he is guilty of blasphemy, because no one is without sin. They are trapped in their own self-righteous attempt to trick Jesus.

No doubt the scribes and Pharisees are shocked and humiliated. They thought this trick would work—they relished their good fortune to find a woman whom they could use as a scapegoat to get Jesus.

But their plan is thwarted. Jesus' focus on human beings rather than strict adherence to law was demoralizing for them. To make matters even worse, Jesus does not rant or rave against them in open confrontation and debate—he simply makes a statement, bends back down and writes.

Jesus challenges their interpretation of the law. Mosaic law was written to govern community life, not to be a trap for persons who understood themselves to be holy and righteous. The scribes and Pharisees had as their concern only the consequences of breaking the law.

They do not care about the woman or her honor. The law seeks compassion and justice for members of the community. This woman is a convenient foil and the men are not interested in rehabilitation or forgiveness. Jesus throws their callousness and viciousness in their faces. Jesus has effectively quieted them and they have no choice but to slink away. None of the men can condemn the woman—no one is without sin. When Jesus stands up the second time, only the woman remains.

He acknowledges and honors her humanity. He addresses her and does not leave her in the past. He, instead, gives her another chance and points toward a future where her humanity is seen and honored. The scribes and Pharisees see her only as an object to be used toward their devious ends. She is not a person in their eyes. Yet in Jesus' eyes, she is a person in need of forgiveness and a second chance. She is part of a community that also knows sin. If her accusers cannot condemn her, neither will Jesus.

Popular interpretation of this story focuses on the grace and forgiveness the woman receives from Jesus. But we must not let her accusers off the hook. The religious leaders have gone to a great deal of trouble to trap Jesus. The men in this story have absolutely *no* regard for this woman.

If the leaders are willing to sacrifice and use this woman, what kind of servants are they for God? How can they, with integrity, talk about God's Realm of justice, compassion, harmony, and love? By challenging the scribes and Pharisees, Jesus challenges the spirit *and* the letter of the law. To ignore one for the sake of the other is failure to adhere to the law. Jesus calls into question both the practiced religion and the patriarchical worldview of the woman's accusers. The remarkable part of this story is the way in which Jesus deals with the trap of the scribes and Pharisees. Jesus' behavior is nothing less than radical. Jesus shames the supposedly honorable men and honors the supposedly shameful woman—he reverses their status.

Jesus' opponents exhibit a mean-spiritedness all too common among some religious folks today. Jesus demonstrates that there is a different way of seeing and being in the world. He forces people to think about what they are doing. In a way, Jesus gives both the accusers and the accused an opportunity for a second chance. The woman can repent and live a life free of the sin of adultery. The men can begin to think in ways that focus on the personhood of each community member. In this way, they can turn from treating people in ways that embarrass and humiliate them.

The accusers were a group of men whose purpose was to entrap Jesus. The law was supposed to provide fair and just treatment for transgressors. In this instance, the law is used against her. Because of Jesus, the law is now used against her accusers. The scribes and Pharisees do a great injustice to the woman; they identify her by only her sin. Jesus illustrates here his understanding of the law and the religious establishment. Rather than view the law only in terms of punishment, Jesus reinterprets the law to hold all accountable and to seek forgiveness and grace. Jesus challenges the political and theological power of the accusers that see death as the only option for transgressions.

The accusers try desperately to cling to the letter of the law to convict Jesus. Jesus stands over and against his opponents by holding them responsible and accountable for their deeds. Jesus offers new life to the woman and the men. This is what makes this story such a powerful one and exposes the accusers as true "bad boys." They behave badly for wrong reasons.

There is much in our society that makes people less than human. Sometimes our attitudes toward others make them feel valueless and unworthy, bothersome and unimportant. Jesus brings a message of human worth and value regardless of gender, color, or station in life.

At the end, Jesus presents opportunities for all of us to start over. In like fashion, Jesus does not leave us stuck in the past. We do not have to stay in places that are demoralizing, humiliating, or dehumanizing. We have the choice to repent and move forward. Surely we must account for our choices and decisions; most often, we must suffer the consequences of our choices. But Jesus makes it clear that we need not stay there forever. Jesus gives us another chance and points us toward a future of freedom and wholeness.

REFLECTION QUESTIONS

1. How do you hold others accountable for their behavior? How do you hold yourself accountable for your own actions?

2. The accusers were not really concerned about punishment for the woman. They were using her to trap Jesus. Have you ever felt used? Explain the situation and tell how you handled it.

3. Have you ever been embarrassed or humiliated in public? Tell how you felt and what you did. If you could relive the situation, what would you do differently?

4. Have you ever been in a no-win situation? What happened? How could you have made it a win-win situation?

5. Some of us "throw stones" at others by telling falsehoods about them or mocking them. What stones do you throw at others? What support do you need to change your behavior?

6. Name and describe institutions that dehumanize people. What can you do to make them more accountable and humane?

7. What attitudes and/or behaviors do you need to change? What hinders you from making the change?

8. How do you define sin? What do you think Jesus would say about your definition?

9. In Jesus' day, who would hear the story of 7:53–8:11 as good news? Who should hear it as good news today?

10. For whom is this story bad news? Explain your answer.

4

THE PHARISEES—PART ONE: THE SYNOPTIC GOSPELS: "NOT AS I DO, BUT AS I SAY!"

"Do not think that I have come to abolish the law or the prophets; I have come not to abolish but to fulfill. For truly I tell you, until heaven and earth pass away, not one letter, not one stroke of a letter, will pass from the law until all is accomplished. (MATT. 5:17–18)

READ MATTHEW 23

The infamous Pharisees are depicted as rigid hypocrites and major adversaries of Jesus. Jesus constantly shows them up and exposes their narrow understanding of the faith. They keep the letter of the law but do not understand its spirit. The Pharisees set into motion the actions leading to Jesus' crucifixion, hoping to squash the growing Jesus movement.

So just who are the dreaded and dreadful Pharisees? Scholars cannot agree, primarily because our sources of information are ambiguous and contradictory. Almost all we know about this group is found in three sources: the New Testament (Christian Scripture), mostly the Gospels and Acts; the works of Jewish historian Josephus; and rabbinic literature. You can tell already that it will be a challenge to untangle truth from fiction.

Most scholars agree that the portrait of the Pharisees in the Gospels is unreliable. The focus of the four Gospels is Jesus—his life, ministry, death, resurrection, and ongoing presence in the church. Any threat to hinder Jesus or his message would be disparaged. Therefore, we should not be surprised that the Pharisees are almost always shown in a negative light. So intense is the case against them that Christians see the

Pharisees as scapegoats for Jesus' execution. However, a closer exam-
ination reveals that much of the antagonism between Jesus and the
Pharisees really reflects the later hostility between established Judaism
and the early church. In Jesus' time and shortly after his crucifixion,
the Jesus movement was seen as a sect of Judaism (and surprise: Jesus
was Jewish, not Christian!). Later, a break between the two left the
church a minority on the religious scene. It took a while for the
Christian church to establish an identity apart from its Jewish roots
and foundation. At the same time, Judaism was reinventing itself after
the destruction of the Temple at Jerusalem in 70 CE. To compound the
challenge, both Judaism and Christianity were busy trying to codify
beliefs and standards in the midst of great pluralism and diversity of
understandings. In other words, during Jesus' day and during the life
of the early church, there was no monolithic Judaism *or* Christianity.
Jews in Jerusalem differed from each other and from Jews in the
Diaspora. Christians differed from each other based on ethnic origin
and geography—Gentile Christians differed from Jewish Christians,
Christians in Jerusalem differed from Christians in Corinth, and so
on—based on geography, culture, education, values, etc.

It is probable that each group sought to make its perspectives and
understandings normative. Naturally, there would be hard feelings
among the groups, each misunderstanding and misrepresenting the
others. Further, it is a short leap to slandering each other and groups
would use whatever rhetorical devices available to discredit the other.
Tragically, these family feuds are evidenced in the anti-Semitic tone of
the Christian Scripture. Unfortunately, the misunderstandings have
lasted into modern times. We will attempt to take a look at a bigger
picture and not perpetuate the myths and fictions that separate Jews
and Christians from each other.

To say that the Gospels are biased against the Pharisees is to make
an understatement. The very name of the Pharisees is shrouded in
mystery. The Greek, *pharisaisos*, is believed to mean "separated ones,"
but this tells us almost nothing about their identity or origins. Some
believe the Pharisees began to codify their understanding of Mosaic

faith after the Exile. It is speculated that the Pharisees belonged to the class of urban artisans who assisted in the Temple building project in Jerusalem. A few scholars think they may have been retainers of the ruling class (middle level officials, bureaucrats, judges, and teachers); we know that some Pharisees held positions on the Sanhedrin but we do not know how extensive their presence was.

The Pharisees tried to set forth a coherent plan of reform. The focus was on living holy and righteous lives as a way to reclaim their position as God's chosen people. Their goal was to live into God's plan of redemption and restoration for Israel. After the Temple was destroyed in 70 CE, the Pharisees exerted great influence on the shape of the faith. Modern Judaism traces its roots back to the reform move-ment of the Pharisees.

The Pharisees in the Synoptic Gospels

The Pharisees are mentioned some 100 times in the New Testament. They are usually shown in opposition to Jesus, although there are instances where Pharisees follow and believe in Jesus and where Jesus is quite friendly with them. The Pharisees are almost invisible in the passion narratives; some scholars see this as evidence of their lack of political power and influence. In addition, there are other groups that oppose Jesus, including the Sadducees, Herodians, scribes, elders, and chief priests. Sometimes, even the Gospel writers seem confused about which groups were in conflict with Jesus at any given time.

The Gospels focus on the life, ministry, death, and resurrection of Jesus of Nazareth. Each Gospel is written for a particular community in order to explain what the Jesus event means in that context. Each Gospel writer stamps the work with a particular spin in order to make the Jesus event relevant. The aim of the Gospels is neither to provide an objective biography of Jesus nor to set forth a critical history of the time. They contain elements of both but are blends of fact and inter-pretation within a framework that always has Jesus as the Christ at its center. What, therefore, we learn about the Pharisees through the Gospels is colored by the context of the writer's community.

The encounters between Jesus and the Pharisees are usually framed within the pattern of a controversy story. Most controversy stories contain some or all of the following elements:

➤ Jesus is observed doing something out of the ordinary or beyond traditional protocol;

➤ Religious men learned in Mosaic law ask a question or pose a challenge for Jesus to address;

➤ Jesus responds by asking a question, expanding or reinterpreting the law at issue;

➤ Religious men are shamed and seek a way to destroy Jesus;

➤ The crowd is amazed or in awe of Jesus' teaching.

Mark provides the general outline for the development of Matthew and Luke. Each Gospel contains materials unique to itself; that is, Matthew has material not found in Mark or Luke; Luke has material not found in Mark or Matthew; and Mark has material not found in Matthew or Luke. So, to explore in detail the ways each Gospel treats the Pharisees quickly results in an unwieldy mess. I encourage you to look at the list of resources at the end of this volume to find works to help you to continue your study of the Pharisees. Having said that, let's take an overview of the Synoptic Gospels' portrait of the Pharisees.

Following Mark's lead, Matthew and Luke present episodes between Jesus and the Pharisees that are not overtly hostile (see Mark 2:13–17; Matt. 9:9–13; Luke 5:27–32). However, the stakes are raised as Jesus continues to defy Mosaic law on various matters: fasting (Matt. 9:14–17; Mark 2:18–22; Luke 5:33–39); Sabbath observance (Matt. 12:9–14; Mark 3:1–6; Luke 6:6–11); marriage and divorce (Matt. 19:1–12; Mark 10:1–12); and ritual purity and cleanness (Matt. 15:1–11; Mark 7:1–13).

At stake in the encounters is the right Jesus claims to interpret the law. His teachings move beyond tradition to interpretations that place human beings at the center. Jesus states that the needs of people are more important than keeping the letter of the law. The Pharisees keep trying to trap Jesus into saying something that will incriminate him with the religious establishment or with the Roman government. They seek to dishonor him as a citizen and to discredit his teaching. Jesus counters and turns their attempts back on them. Both must find ways to restore their honor. Jesus does a much better job at this than the Pharisees.

It is important to remind ourselves here that the Pharisees were not doing anything wrong from their perspective. Remember that their focus was on the "right living" of Mosaic law. Their job was to make sure that the law was rightly interpreted so the people could reclaim their place of honor in God's eyes. They had every right to investigate any and all new teachings that did not closely adhere to the established orthodoxy (or what they considered orthodoxy). Failure to do their job would have resulted in all kinds of blasphemies and accommodations to compromises.

As a charismatic leader and teacher, Jesus posed a real concern for the established religious authority. Jesus had not been sanctioned by anyone who had the power to do so. That Jesus proved a worthy opponent only compounded the problem. As the Pharisees checked out Jesus, they had no intentions early on to get rid of him. As interpreters of the law, the Pharisees were open to hearing various viewpoints— they had no problem with that. If Jesus had been exposed as a charlatan or false teacher, he would have faded into the background as the people ignored him. But Jesus understood the law as deeply as the Pharisees and he cut to the heart of God's intention for humanity. The Pharisees' mission was to make sure the people understood the law so they could live holy lives that were wholly acceptable to God. They may not have paid much attention to Jesus had he stayed within established limits. Indeed the Pharisees knew and understood the importance of recognizing and responding to human needs—but who gave *Jesus* the right to do so? Jesus hung out and even dined with toll collectors and sinners—he already violated the marks of a holy and righteous life—what right did he have to tell others what to do? It seemed as though Jesus held to some laws and defied others—how reliable could his teachings be? To top it all off, Jesus has the audacity to challenge the authority of the Pharisees—in the synagogue, of all places!

Jesus actually left the Pharisees no choice but to find ways to get rid of him. For the Pharisees, the very life of the faith was at stake. The established orthodoxy had history, scripture, and experience on their side; Jesus was just one person who rose up out of nowhere—Nazareth, no less—and he claimed to know the heart and mind of God. Far from being fanatical, the Pharisees had to protect the faith, as they knew it.

If, indeed, Jesus was in direct conflict with the Pharisees, we see the tension most intensely in Matt. 23:1–36. Matthew follows Mark's outline (Mark 12:37b–40) but includes material not found in Mark. Some of Matthew's material is found in various places in Luke (20:45–47; 11:46, 52; 11:39–42, 47–51). Matthew uses the Pharisees to warn his own community through a series of seven woes.

In Matthew 23, Jesus addresses the crowds and his disciples. The scribes are a professional group of men steeped in Mosaic law. They are often paired with the Pharisees and other groups in opposition to Jesus. Jesus acknowledges the authority of the scribes and Pharisees as that of the establishment. Jesus warns that they do not practice what they preach and teach. He states that *what* they teach is fine, but *they* are not good role models of their own teaching.

In Matthew 23:13–36, we find the seven "woes" upon the scribes and Pharisees although they are not a substantial (if any) part of the gathered crowd. The descriptions in the woes have added fuel to the anti-Semitic undertones all too prevalent in the Gospels and in Christianity. Let's explore the woes and briefly see what they may really mean; most of this material is from the Q source that Matthew adapts:

➤ In Matthew 23:13, the scribes and Pharisees are about the business of getting into heaven but their tactics, seemingly nitpicky rules and regulations, keep them and others out of God's Kingdom; rather than opening the way to God, they effectively close the way to those who want to enter. Their tradition is exclusive rather than radically inclusive, which characterizes God's Kingdom/Realm. Consistently, we see Jesus expanding the range of those to be included in God's household: the outcasts, women, toll collectors, and sinners.

➤ In Matthew 23:15, the scribes and Pharisees require would-be converts to become fully Jewish—which means men must be circumcised and must embrace Mosaic law. Matthew's church had an active Gentile mission but did not require converts to become thoroughly Jewish for membership (a tension also found in the churches founded by Paul). In other words, for the scribes and Pharisees, the convert had to be "more Jewish than Jews" in order to belong within the circle of God's care. They felt that Israel was still God's chosen people. If any were to be included in God's household, they must be from the house of Israel. In effect, they were converting people more to Pharisaism rather than to Judaism in general. Remember that there was no solid, monolithic entity of Judaism at that time. The Pharisees taught what they knew and believed to be the right way. In their system, some were included which means that some were excluded.

➤ In Matthew 23:16–22, the scribes and Pharisees are called on what makes a valid oath and what does not. They are accused of stating things so that loopholes can be found and exploited when it is expedient to do so. Valid oaths usually included the name of God. God, then, becomes a partner in the transaction and one is bound to the terms of the oath (see the story of Jephthah in *Bad Boys of the Bible: Exploring Men of Questionable Virtue*, 2002). The Pharisees provided ways to get around the consequences of an oath when they needed to.

➤ In Matthew 23:23–24, they are accused of sacrificing material goods at the expense of more important wealth—spiritual values and behaviors. They readily tithe their agricultural goods, but fail to "tithe" justice, mercy, and faithfulness to uphold the essence of the law. In their zeal to make sure they tithe even the most insignificant of their riches, they neglect the really important thing—showing to their brothers and sisters the love, care, and concern that God intends for human community. So instead, they are too often unjust, arrogant, cruel, unmerciful, and unloving. They are so focused on little things that they miss the big ones.

➤ In Matthew 23:25–26, they are depicted as caring more about outward expressions than about inward integrity and uprightness. If all actions have their genesis in the heart, then we would do well to get our inside cleaned up before we act. The warning here is to integrate and balance one's inward thoughts and outward actions.

➤ In Matthew 23:27–28, the image of whitewashed tombs makes little sense to us. Let us remember that ancient highways and roads were carved through hills and were not like the super highways that we know. Along the roads, tombs would be carved into the hills where bones were interred. Touching a tomb rendered one ritually unclean (see Samson's story in *Bad Boys of the Bible: Exploring Men of Questionable Virtue*, 2002)— *Those who touch the dead body of any human being shall be unclean seven days. They shall purify themselves with the water on the third day and on the seventh day, and so be clean; but if they do not purify themselves on the third day and on the seventh day, they will not become clean. All who touch a corpse, the body of a human being who has died, and do not purify themselves, defile the tabernacle of the LORD; such persons shall be cut off from Israel. Since water for cleansing was not dashed on them, they remain unclean; their uncleanness is still on them.* (Numbers 19:11–13) As a sign to travelers, tombs were marked with white paint so they could be avoided. This was a kind of public service especially for those making the pilgrimage to Jerusalem for Passover. Contamination along the way would exclude the pilgrim from participating in the festival. The image is striking—the tombs look pretty on the outside but are rotten on the inside—just like the scribes and Pharisees.

➤ In Matthew 23:29–36, the scribes and Pharisees are shown as the descendents of those who persecuted and killed God's prophets of the Hebrew Bible. The scribes and Pharisees build monuments to honor and commemorate God's slain messengers. Further the scribes and

Pharisees declare that they would never have killed God's prophets. But Jesus knows better—given the same situation where they were to be challenged, they would do as their ancestors. Their monuments are not suitable reparation for the actions of their ancestors—in fact, they have not learned anything from history. They continue to persecute God's prophets—John the Baptist, Jesus, and others to follow. The scribes and Pharisees are made of the same cloth as their ancestors—getting rid of that which irritates and threatens, no matter how accurate the indictment by the prophets. The scribes and Pharisees have effectively sealed their fate. They are doomed because they fail to recognize God's messengers and they fail to heed God's message through them. While the scribes and Pharisees feel they have heaven all sewn up for themselves, Jesus tells them they do not. They have human blood on their hands—from Abel to Zechariah—the first and the last murdered in the Hebrew Bible and they must pay for this.

Wow! So, what are we to make of all this? First, it is interesting to note that Mark includes no woes in his Gospel; and Luke includes two in which the Pharisees are specifically named (Luke 11:39; 11:42).

Matthew did not see his community as distinctly separated from the Jewish community. His Gospel is steeped in Israel's scripture and ethos. His concerns for Mosaic law, Sabbath, and ritual purity are thoroughly Jewish. The Matthean church was obviously in some tension with the established religious leadership of his day. Jesus was the Messiah, God's promised redeemer for Israel. Thus, Matthew's community was in line with Judaism, not in opposition to it. However, we cannot define with certainty what "it" was—Judaism was as fluid at that time as the emerging Christian movement. It is naïve, though, to think that Matthew's community lived peacefully with whatever forms of Judaism were operative at the time. It is believed that the Matthean church broke with Judaism to carry its message and mission to the Gentile world. For Matthew, his community comprised the true people of God, which found itself in conflict with the emerging established Judaism and was persecuted by the religious authority.

However, his opposition to Judaism must not be used as fuel for anti-Semitism. In fact, in many ways and on several issues, Matthew's is a family fight. It is only after he recognizes that reform is not an option that Matthew's mission shifts to the Gentiles.

Thus, the woes in Matthew 23 are not designed to denigrate the scribes and Pharisees, per se. They are not angry railings of Jesus against the leaders of his day. Rather, Matthew uses the woes as warnings to his own community as it seeks to establish its identity and its own brand of orthodoxy. Given its Jewish roots and its current situation in a pluralistic and diverse world, what does the Matthean church have to be and do in order to distinguish itself from others? Matthew encourages his community to understand the spirit of Mosaic law. The community must live by the principles of justice, mercy, and faithfulness; must interact with each other with integrity and honesty; must honor God's messengers; must live as people of God who embrace Jesus as God's Messiah. Matthew warns them to live out God's intention because if they don't, they will suffer the fate of their ancestors—annihilation and/or exile.

Mark's treatment of the Pharisees is less intense than Matthew's. Mark refers to the Pharisees as hypocrites once (Mark 7:1–8), but tensions between Jesus and the Pharisees escalate as Jesus continues to challenge the human tradition of the Pharisees. Their issues with Jesus focus on his choice of dinner companions (toll collectors and sinners, Mark 2:15–17); fasting (Mark 2:18–22); Sabbath keeping (Mark 2:24–3:16); ritual cleanliness (Mark 7:1–8); divorce (Mark 10:2–9); and tribute to Caesar (Mark 12:13–17). The basic problem has to do with Jesus' authority to interpret and teach the law. In the eyes of the scribes and Pharisees, Jesus is an upstart from a backwater town who has not been sanctioned to preach or teach. Further, his interpretation expands the law to make it "customer friendly." That is, Jesus makes the prospect of holiness as a lifestyle accessible to a wide range of outcasts—toll collectors, women, the infirmed, and sinners. Even more, Jesus forgives sin and creates a future for people who are as good as dead as far as the established religious systems are concerned.

In Luke, there is a mixed bag of interaction between Jesus and the Pharisees. We meet the scribes and Pharisees when Jesus heals a man whose friends remove a roof to lower him into the house so Jesus might heal him (Luke 5:17–26). The scribes and Pharisees have come from every village in Galilee and Judea to hear Jesus preach. It is not clear whether they are there to test Jesus or if they are there because they are simply interested in hearing what he has to say. Jesus forgives the paralyzed man's sins; the scribes and Pharisees accuse Jesus of blasphemy, a serious charge. Blasphemy was akin to making oneself equal to God; the penalty—stoning to death (Leviticus 24:10–16). The crowd is amazed as Jesus teaches, heals, and forgives the sins of the man. We suspect that tension between Jesus and the scribes and Pharisees will grow.

In the next episode between Jesus and his opponents, we find Jesus eating with all the wrong people—toll collectors and sinners (Luke 5:27–32). The animosity between the toll collectors and Pharisees was deep. Toll collectors were despised because they cheated people for a profit. The Pharisees were meticulous keepers of the law and wanted to associate only with those who practiced the faith as they did. It was bad enough that Jesus saw fit to eat with toll collectors, but he called one to be his disciple! The Pharisees complained about Jesus to express their shock and disbelief—Jesus is way over the top in his associations with undesirable people.

The conflict heightens in the very next scene about fasting (Luke 5:33–39). For the Christian community, celebration took precedence over fasting although there is a place for fasting. Jesus' community was about feasting and breaking bread together, a tradition that continues and characterizes Christian fellowship. The next scene continues to build suspense as Jesus is confronted about the Sabbath (Luke 6:1–11). Things are totally out of control and Jesus is in trouble: *But they were filled with fury and discussed with one another what they might do to Jesus* (LUKE 6:11).

Jesus is depicted as ushering in a new world order, one that values human need over tradition. Jesus constantly explains why he or his disciples behave in certain ways. Jesus lifts up examples of violations in Israel's history. Jesus claims the same authority as that of David and the prophets to do the right thing for the right reason—paying more attention to human need over traditional rituals (see Mark 2:27). What is more, Jesus heals the man with the withered hand on the Sabbath, knowing that the scribes and Pharisees are watching. They seek a way to get rid of Jesus—on the Sabbath! How ironic that Jesus is about healing and restoring health while his opponents are about harming and removing Jesus.

In Luke 7:36–50, Jesus accepts a dinner invitation from Simon the Pharisee; encounters an unnamed woman who anoints him with ointment; and uses a parable to teach about the forgiveness of sin. The episode with the woman parallels episodes in all the other Gospels; but Luke makes significant changes. For example, in Matthew (26:6–13), Mark (14:3–9), and John (12:1–8), the setting for the encounter is in Galilee during the earlier part of Jesus' ministry. In the other Gospels, the encounter takes place in Bethany during the Passover season. Here in Luke, the story is not linked with the anointing or burial of Jesus. Luke, instead, links the story with love and forgiveness. Scholars are undecided on how to reconcile the differences—either Luke used an actual event in Jesus' ministry or he confused details of Mark's account or there were two such events in Jesus' ministry. The point Luke seems to make is that Jesus was not opposed to interacting with outcasts—toll collectors, women, and sinners.

There is great tension in this passage on a number of levels. First, the dinner party would have been of great interest to the townspeople. A banquet would have been a more public affair than dinners to which we may be accustomed. People would have been able to crowd around Simon's house and see the proceedings.

Secondly, guests did not sit in chairs at a table; instead, they reclined on their left sides in order to eat with their right hand. Their feet would have been spread away from the mat where the food was placed. The woman would have had easy access to Jesus' feet. The woman's tears fall upon Jesus' feet, and she uses her hair to dry them.

She then kisses and anoints his feet. She engages in a seemingly spontaneous act of love and thankfulness although we don't know the basis for her actions. She totally disregards social protocol—touching or caressing a man's feet carried sexual implications. Add to this her sinful state and that she touched Jesus, which then made him ritually unclean.

Thirdly, Simon is concerned about the woman's scandalous behavior. Jesus points out that Simon himself has violated hospitality protocol. Simon did not extend to Jesus: water with which to wash his feet; a kiss of greeting and peace; oil with which to anoint his head. Jesus addresses Simon's *faux pas* and elevates the woman's—Jesus is more than a prophet (which Simon questions) because he knows the heart, mind, and character of both Simon and the woman. Jesus forgives the woman's sin and shames Simon because of his partial hospitality and judgment of the woman.

We next see Jesus eating with Pharisees in Luke 11:37–54. Jesus fails to wash his hands before taking his place at the dinner table. The Pharisee is amazed but he doesn't say anything. But Jesus uses the occasion to utter woes against the Pharisees and lawyers. Again, there are parallels to Matthew 23 but with significant differences here. The episode serves to intensify the conflict between Jesus and the scribes and Pharisees who are now actively seeking to entrap him (Luke 11:53–54). The purpose of the woe is to serve as a warning to those who would follow Jesus—live the spirit *and* the letter of the law.

In Luke 14:1–6, Jesus dines with a leader of the Pharisees on the Sabbath, despite the fact that Jesus knows the scribes and Pharisees are watching him closely. Jesus heals a man of dropsy and challenges the traditional understanding of Sabbath observance. Jesus silences his opponents (14:6).

We have seen Pharisees extending table fellowship to Jesus. In each case, the meal was an occasion to deepen the conflict between Jesus and the Pharisees. Yet they invite Jesus to dine with them, a sincere sign of hospitality. And Jesus accepts their invitations. So it is difficult to say that Jesus was at odds with all scribes and Pharisees. Further, in Luke, the Pharisees disappear from the passion narrative although they have members on the Sanhedrin, the council of Jewish leaders who hear the case against Jesus (Matt. 26:59–60; Mark 14:55–56; Luke 22:66).

In Luke, the Pharisees provide a link between Israel's history and legacy and the emerging church. Christian faith is an authentic expression of Jewish faith, as Luke understands it. In the Book of Acts, the Pharisees are respected and are sympathetic to Christian perspectives (see Acts 5:34–40, 15:5).

The Pharisees set up a picture of God's Realm (Kingdom) that excludes persons for various reasons. Jesus teaches about a kingdom in opposition to theirs. For Jesus, God's Realm includes the poor, the maimed, the blind, the lame, toll collectors, women, and sinners—all who make a decision to accept God. Folks like the Pharisees feel they can get into God's Realm on their religious behavior alone and thereby they opt out of God's invitation (see the unit on the Elder Brother). They fail to see God's inbreaking (through the person and ministry of John the Baptist and Jesus) and effectively close themselves off from God's salvation.

REFLECTION QUESTIONS

1. How has your opinion of the Pharisees changed by studying this unit?

2. What are your core values? Name four and tell why they are important to you.

3. Is it possible to stand firmly in what you believe and allow others to do the same if they differ from you? Are there examples of people peacefully coexisting in the world today? Name and celebrate them.

4. What is the difference between commitment and fanaticism?

5. How are beliefs, traditions, and values transmitted in your family? In your church? Who determines what gets passed on?

6. What stories shape who you are, how you believe, and how you behave in the world? Relate one story that illustrates this.

7. How can the church be sure of someone's "call" to service and/or ministry? What should be the test for authenticity?

8. How do you handle conflict? How does your church handle conflict? What support do you and/or your church need to deal with conflict in constructive ways?

9. There are times when the Pharisees seem interested and fascinated with Jesus. Why do you think they later turn on him and plot to kill him?

10. Who doesn't get it—Jesus or the Pharisees? Explain your answer. What is really at stake for the Pharisees? For Jesus?

5

THE PHARISEES—PART TWO: THE GOSPEL OF JOHN AND EXTRA BIBLICAL SOURCES: "LET'S PLAY FAMILY FEUD!"

THE PHARISEES IN THE GOSPEL OF JOHN

READ JOHN 7:14–52

In John, the Pharisees are one of several groups of religious leaders. By the time of John's writing, the Pharisees were the dominant influence on Judaism. Jesus' relationship to the religious authorities of his day evolves from a fairly mild one to one of hostility. In John's Gospel, Jesus engages them in a conversation that widens the gulf between them. John's community was in great conflict with the synagogue. In fact, the Christian community had been cast out of the synagogue and was persecuted by their Jewish brothers and sisters. Much of John's Gospel exposes the pain of his community at being cut off from its Jewish roots, history, and legacy. The animosity against the "Jews" is a venting of pain and hurt and is not to be construed as anti-Semitic. John does not identify who the "Jews" are but scholars include the Pharisees among the opponents of Jesus.

We see the Pharisees early in Jesus' ministry when an envoy is sent; they question John the Baptist about his testimony and actions. Jesus' first encounter with them is recorded in 3:1–21. A leader of the Pharisees, Nicodemus, visits Jesus in the night. Nicodemus and Jesus engage in a theological discussion about being born again. Nicodemus speaks for other religious leaders here; he is respectful and he seems genuinely interested in Jesus' response. Jesus then launches into one of his long theological discourses so prevalent in John's Gospel. This is the only place in John where a reference is made to "kingdom of God." Jesus teaches Nicodemus that being born again opens a new dimension to God. Nicodemus, though, doesn't get it and Jesus tries to explain:

new birth comes from water and Spirit. What Nicodemus presumed to know (v. 2), is what Jesus makes apparent that he *does not* know— the workings of God in ushering in a new Realm (Kingdom); Nicodemus approaches Jesus at night and remains in the dark.

In chapters seven and eight, the hostility between Jesus and the Pharisees/Jews continues to escalate. Jesus identifies himself as one who is sent from God (7:16, 28–29, 33; 8:16, 18, 29, 42). Further, Jesus is clear that he is teaching an honest interpretation of Jewish law (7:22–23, 47–52; 8:39–41, 52–58). Jesus' teachings demand a decision for Jesus against the world (7:31, 40–44; 8:30–33, 42–43, 47). As would be expected, the plot to kill Jesus heats up (7:1, 13, 19, 25, 30, 32, 44; 8:37, 40, 59). His opponents are mainly the "Jews" but the Pharisees are also named: 7:32, 45–52; 8:3–11 (see chapter on the Accusers of the Woman Caught in Adultery); 8:13–20.

In John 9:13–17, the Pharisees question the man who was healed of blindness by Jesus on the Sabbath. The officials question his parents about the situation. This incident contains the gist of the Fourth Gospel towards the "Jews"—*His parents . . . were afraid of the Jews; for the Jews had already agreed that anyone who confessed Jesus to be the Messiah would be put out of the synagogue.* (JOHN 9:22)

They question the man again and then drive him out of the synagogue. In contrast to the religious authorities, Jesus finds the man and asks him about his beliefs—see John 9:35–38. Some Pharisees overhear the conversation and want to know if Jesus thinks they, too, are blind. Jesus says, plainly, yes, they are because they fail to see that God sent Jesus. For John, this incident in the ministry of Jesus mirrors the Johannine situation.

After Jesus raises Lazarus from death in John 11:1–44, the religious authorities feel an urgency to kill Jesus, at an opportune time:

Many of the Jews therefore, who had come with Mary and had seen what Jesus did, believed in him. But some of them went to the Pharisees and told them what he had done. So the chief priests and the Pharisees called a meeting of the council, and said, "What are we to do? This man is performing many signs. If we let him go on like this, everyone will believe in him, and the Romans will come and destroy both our holy place and our nation." JOHN 11:45–48

The Pharisees, while having no official power to call a meeting of the Sanhedrin, had a voice since many of the scribes were also Pharisees. John's community was in conflict with the heirs of the Pharisees— there is fluidity in the use of the terms "Pharisees" and "Jews" in John's Gospel. The Sanhedrin seeks to preserve their political well-being spurred by the Pharisees' religious concern. The power base of the Sanhedrin is at stake, while for the Pharisees, the very faith of their ancestors is at stake. The decision to kill Jesus is now officially sanctioned. The Sanhedrin thinks its decision to assassinate Jesus will end the Jesus movement. Instead, they play right into God's plan for salvation. They will not take Jesus' life; Jesus will lay down his life in his own time and in his own way.

The Pharisees are mentioned in John 12:19 and 42; but Jesus does not interact with them again until he is arrested (18:3).

It is important to revisit John's treatment of Jesus' opponents. John presents Jesus as a Jewish native of Nazareth. The conflict is between those who believe that Jesus is the Messiah and those who do not. In addition, those who oppose Jesus look but do not see; they listen but do not hear; they ask questions but do not understand; they witness miracles but ask for signs. For John, those who do not believe have no place in the community. It is not possible to identify just who the "Jews" are and, certainly, we cannot categorically link them to modern Jews. In the Gospel, the opponents of Jesus include the Pharisees, scribes, chief priests, and elders—none of whom are clearly identified. We know that on some level, they collectively represent the religious authority.

The "Jews" are anxiously awaiting the arrival of God's Messiah. They picture one who possesses political and military power, on the order of King David. They do not expect the Messiah to reinterpret or expand the centerpiece of their faith—Mosaic law. The synagogue is the place where the scripture is heard and interpreted. There is a need to keep the faith pure and teachings consistent. The life of the community is mediated, shaped, and governed by God's words in the Hebrew Bible (we don't get a "New Testament" until after Jesus' resurrection). The scripture—law and the prophets—form the standard for life in the Jewish community. When conflicts need mediation or decisions to be made, the authorities go to the scripture, the arbiter of justice for Jews.

John's community sees in Jesus the fulfillment of scripture and God's intention for God's people. Jesus is the Messiah! This community continues to practice aspects of Judaism while living out their faith in Jesus. The dual alliance causes some tension between synagogue and church. The synagogue wants indisputable proof that Jesus is the Messiah. Much of John's Gospel attempts to "prove" to Jewish leaders that Jesus is, indeed, God's Anointed One.

When the Jews threaten to cut off the church, John's community is thrown into a panic. For the descendants of Israel, covenant is all about community. There is no life without community; people are identified by bloodlines and not as individuals (that is why people remarked about where Jesus was from and who his people were). To be cast out was a fate worse than death. The tribes of Israel, despite their issues, saw themselves as connected to one another in real and powerful ways. God related to them as a group (as Jesus relates to the church) and to be cut off from the group was to be cut off from God. It was a serious matter for the believers in the God of Abraham, Isaac, and Jacob to be in community.

John's community believed fervently that Jesus was God's Messiah and that put them in opposition to their sisters and brothers in the synagogue, who are labeled generically as the "Jews." The Jews saw John's community as a subversive group of misguided folks who blasphemed against God by believing in a carpenter from Nazareth. Their own relatives and faith community ostracized the Johannine community. They saw themselves as outcasts, rejected and cut off from the family within which they found their identity. They saw themselves as powerless victims of the dominant religious group of which they had been a part all their lives. The "Jews" were not inherently bad people; they were attempting to keep their traditions intact and pure. They do not fall for the claims of each and every teacher who comes along—Israel's history is replete with false teachers and false prophets. Until they have proof, Jesus is just another in a long line of would-be prophets and teachers of God. The goal of the Jews was not to hurt Jesus or his followers, unless they were forced to do so.

Jesus' mission was public and challenged the basic tenets of Judaism. He did not try to do away with the law, but his interpretations stretched the limits of the known orthodoxy. He healed on the Sabbath, he hung out with sinners and women, and he gave hope to the hopeless. Jesus, in his boldness, captured the imaginations of a people whose hope was dormant, where it existed at all. And what is more, Jesus awakened the personal power of common people. Those who had been afflicted their entire lives now danced and lived in wholeness. Those who had been isolated and neglected now knew love and care and community. Those who lived in the shadows of shame and guilt and sin now held their heads high; those who mourned now rejoiced. Those who were despised by the "Jews" now had worth and value. The Fourth Gospel is the story of those who were cut off; it is not the story of the dominant group in power. The voice here is that of those whose power is not of this world; the world had turned against it.

The issues emphasized in John 7 and 8 are important ones: the (right) interpretation of Mosaic law, the credibility of witnesses to Jesus' identity and familial ties to Abraham. They represent family struggles for clarity. It is a mistake to think that this struggle mirrors modern religious conflicts. We cannot take the tone of these chapters and use it as a weapon against Jews today. The situation of that time was different and the result of different motives. Christians are no longer a minority of Judaism; Christianity is a major player on the stage of world religions. The function of John 7 and 8 is to bolster the community's self-esteem and to point out the error of non-believers.

So now, where are we on the matter of the bad boy Pharisees? The Gospels describe them as self-serving, arrogant, mean-spirited persons who simply do not practice what they preach. They concentrate on outward behavior as a sign of genuine holiness and faithfulness to God's law. There is some validity to their position. God called Israel to be different from the other nations and peoples of the world. The only way Israel could show that it was different was in how they interacted among themselves and with those outside the community. It was important, therefore, that they behave in ways that set them apart from others.

The Pharisees sought to make sure that their people reclaimed their calling to be different. Their mission was to make sure people knew what they were supposed to do because their future depended on right behavior. Mosaic law laid down the foundation for behavior for every aspect of life. So naturally, the Pharisees, as upholders of the law, would be concerned about issues of food, fasting, prayer, worship, family, ritual purity, and Sabbath keeping.

For the Pharisees, the very survival of the faith was at stake. They were human beings whose hope was that God would reclaim them as God's chosen people. The problem was that their zeal sent them on a path that lost sight of their real mission. In their effort to regulate the faith and establish orthodoxy, a standard, they may have gone overboard—at least, that is how Jesus saw it. Their hearts were in the right place, but their methods may have gotten in the way.

We see that early in his ministry, Jesus evoked curiosity and questioning but not outright hostility. As Jesus continued his teaching, he alienated himself from the established Jewish authorities among who were a number of Pharisees. The gap between Jesus and them widened as Jesus opened up a new way of understanding and living Mosaic law. Jesus' understanding of God's Realm (Kingdom) differed vastly from the Pharisees'. For Jesus, God's household included toll collectors, sinners, and women—all who have no place in a Pharisaic realm. For Jesus, God's Realm is radically inclusive and at odds with earthly kingdoms.

The Pharisees, though searching for the Messiah, fail to see God at work in their midst through the humble carpenter from Nazareth.

Their focus was on preserving the faith whose center was the law and the prophets. They sought reforms that would recapture and reclaim covenant ties with the God of Abraham, Isaac, and Jacob.

The Gospel writers write to remind their communities that God is doing a new thing. They don't have to wait any longer because God has sent the Messiah. And what a Messiah he is! Jesus heals the sick, feeds the hungry, forgives sin, raises the dead, and preaches Good News to those oppressed by powers and principalities. Jesus gives hope, light, second chances, and new leases on life.

The Jews and early Christians were jockeying for position and identity. They did horrible things and said even more horrible things to and about each other in their efforts to stand their ground. The rhetoric of the Gospels is intended to get one up on those who do not believe Jesus is God's Anointed One promised in the law and the prophets. The wording and the tone of the Gospels are designed to bolster fledging and marginalized communities. The language is over the top on purpose and not an indictment on the groups in opposition to them. And remember, we never hear the Pharisees defend themselves against their portrait in the Gospels. And the rhetoric of the Gospels is not tempered by extrabiblical sources

The Pharisees in Josephus and Rabbinic Literature

Flavius Josephus was a Jewish historian who lived and wrote during the first century CE. He claimed to be a Pharisee, born into a priestly family. During the rebellion against Rome (66 CE), he led forces against Rome in Galilee. He was captured and taken to Rome where he lived out his days writing. Four of his works survive: *The Jewish War*, a seven-volume collection on the Jewish revolt and historical survey of Jewish history; *The Antiquities of the Jews*, a twenty-volume summary of Jewish scripture and post-biblical Jewish history; *Against Apion*, a two-volume collection supporting Jews against slander during the Hellenistic period; and *Life*, a supplement to *The Antiquities* that is autobiographical in nature, chronicling his revolutionary leadership in Galilee.

He gives a mixed picture of the Pharisees. On the one hand, he praises them for their piety and influence among the people. He tells stories of their oppression. He relates stories about their victim status. On the other hand, he depicts them as rebellious against Roman authority. His primary purpose is to justify their existence to the Roman world; thus, much of his work is apologetic. It is not clear just who the Pharisees are from his description of their actions.

Rabbinic literature was codified after about 200 CE. This body of literature highlights two schools of Jewish thought—Shammai and Hillel. The concerns of these ways of thinking include ritual purity, tithing, and Sabbath observance—issues that also concerned Jesus earlier. Modern rabbis trace their roots back to Pharisaic reform and thus show the Pharisees in a most flattering light. The Pharisees are men of intellect whose roots are in the oral and written law. They are devoted and loyal religious men. There are some who rebel against the government; in rabbinic literature, they are exceptions rather than the rule when it comes to Pharisaism. What we can know with more certainty is that the Pharisees were instrumental in the development of modern Judaism.

Given the biased nature of our sources, we are not able to paint any kind of objective or clear picture of the Pharisees. We have partial pictures of religious rivals going at each other with contradictory and stereotypical images. We must question the pictures of them that we find in the Gospels. Much of the tensions in those texts are reflective of the early church's issues rather than Jesus' issues with his opponents. Thus, the Gospels give us a biased, uncritical, and, in cases, inaccurate picture which has led to Christian anti-Semitism.

We are left with portrayals of defective characters who are self-centered, selfish, mercenary, greedy, uncaring, callous, ruthless, cruel, showy, and concerned more with externals. But we are cautioned against making any conclusions about the Pharisees. Most of what we learn is not personal, but an attempt by the Gospel writers to accurately portray their own contexts and situations against the backdrop of the Christ event. The Gospels spell out differences between Jesus and the Jews, to be sure. But more, the Gospels seek to inform, remind, edify, and inspire the communities that gave birth to the Gospels.

Some scholars see the spurious language of the Gospels as a literary device rather than theological indictments and I think they are correct. There is no denying that Jesus was thoroughly Jewish. Had the authorities been open to earnest reform and thorough investigation, the Jesus movement would have flourished within Judaism and there would have been no need for a Christian church. But the difference could not be held in a Jewish system itself struggling for a sense of identity and for a center. Some tried to straddle both Jewish and Christian worlds—but as both faith traditions grew and spread throughout the world, a break was inevitable. In the Gospels, we find communities struggling with their Jewish sisters and brothers to understand what Jesus did in challenging their eschatological hopes, their understandings about food, ritual, and limits and sources of authority.

It was the duty of the Pharisees to set standards. So what were they to do with an unknown charismatic preacher, teacher, and healer who worked miracles, forgave sins, and always put lowly people first? How were they to contain the carpenter from a no-count village who claimed familial connection to the God who delivered Israel out of Egyptian bondage and set them on a course toward nationhood, freedom, and glory? How were they to maintain control over a religious man who continually violated social and religious protocol and decorum? What were they to do with a man who understood the law and prophets better than those who had dedicated their lives to interpreting the faith? What were they to do with one who shamed them with their own narrow understandings of God's workings in the world?

The Pharisees were faced with a tough dilemma. Their attempts to discredit Jesus just didn't work. Jesus wouldn't be quiet and wouldn't go away. He exercised power and authority that was beyond the Pharisees' capacity to understand or accept. We are left wondering how bad the Pharisees actually were. They were simply trying to save their synagogue from false teachers who swayed people away from

God. For the Pharisees, adherence to the law was the thing that most distinguished them from others. That the Pharisees greatly influenced modern rabbinic faith is a testament to their earnest mission of passing on their faith.

Now, what is your opinion—bad boys or not?

REFLECTION QUESTIONS

1. Do you believe in conspiracy theories? Why or why not? Does the story of Jesus' opponents change your mind about conspiracies?

2. The conflict between Jesus and the Pharisees is colored by the convergence of religion and politics. What modern conflicts mirror this same convergence? What should be done about it?

3. Is Jesus a victim or an agent in his death? Explain your answer.

4. What stereotypes of the Pharisees do we find in the Gospels? Have you ever been stereotyped? In what ways? What can you do about it?

5. How do you deal with competition? What is the difference between competition and rivalry? Explain.

6. What could Jesus and the Pharisees have done to get along better with each other?

7. How should the church deal with charismatic, popular teachers and preachers who defy protocol?

8. In what ways does the church need to change in order to be radically inclusive?

9. Do you stereotype others? How do you think they feel about that?

10. The conflict between John's community and the synagogue is a family fight. Are there modern family feuds that mirror the biblical conflict? Explain.

6

JUDAS ISCARIOT: "I DID IT FOR US!"

Even my bosom friend in whom I trusted, who ate of my bread, has lifted the heel against me. (PSALM 41:9)

READ MATTHEW 27:3–10 AND JOHN 18:1–12

Judas Iscariot has been demonized beyond belief. Like Jezebel's, his very name conjures up images of betrayal and treachery. He is always named last in the lists of Twelve Jesus called to his inner circle. Almost always, he is identified as the one who betrays Jesus. Does Judas have any redeeming qualities?

We can never know what was in the heart and mind of Judas. What little we know of him is sketchy, episodic, and biased from beginning to end. How must it feel to always be known as the one who betrayed Jesus?

Judas has troubled me for decades because his story doesn't make a lot of sense. Why on earth would *anyone* do what he did? Judas was called and chosen by Jesus to share in his life and ministry; was commissioned and sent out to do works of service and healing; had the privilege of dining and partying with Jesus; witnessed Jesus' mighty acts and wonders. What is more, Judas heard Jesus' words about commitment, loyalty, faithfulness, and integrity—how on earth did Judas miss the point of it all? But then again, maybe Judas understood all too well the point of it all—ultimately, God is to be glorified. Let us explore Judas' story for some clues that might help us be better disciples.

Matthew has two early call narratives. In the first (4:18–22), Jesus walks by the Sea of Galilee and extends an invitation to Simon (also called Peter) and his brother Andrew, James (son of Zebedee) and his brother John. Jesus takes the initiative and seeks out the men who are busy with their regular work routines. There are no dramatic, earth-shattering events—Jesus sees, speaks, calls, and promises: "Follow me, and I will make you fish for people . . . " The four men leave their work to follow Jesus; this reminds us of Abraham's call (see Genesis 12:1–9). Abraham's life is disrupted by a call and command that seems to come out of the blue. Yet, the authority of the call and command is enough to make Abraham go; and the four fisherpersons do likewise at the voice of Jesus.

Matthew's second call narrative is found at 9:9 where Jesus calls Matthew, a toll collector. Again, the interaction between Jesus and Matthew is short, sweet, and to the point, "Follow me." Matthew obeys without question. We have a hint here that Jesus is working out-side the box. Fishing was a respectable career choice in Jesus' day. But collecting tolls was not. In fact, some of the most despised people in society were the toll collectors. They were seen as dishonest exploiters. They were in constant contact with Gentiles and were seen as ritually unclean. Often in the Gospels, tax and toll collectors are linked with sinners. That Jesus calls a toll collector to be part of his inner circle is a huge deal. If Jesus calls the dreaded toll collector, whom else might Jesus call?

So far, Jesus has five disciples: Simon (Peter), Andrew, James, John, and Matthew. When we get to Matthew 10, we learn that there are twelve disciples. Matthew lists them but doesn't give us much back-ground information on the men; in addition to the five, he names Philip, Bartholomew, Thomas, James (son of Alphaeus), Thaddeus, Simon (the Cananaean) and Judas Iscariot . . . *the one who betrayed Jesus.* We do, however, learn something interesting about two of them. The second Simon is the "Cananaean." This connects him to the Zealots. At that time, though, the group had not evolved into a later revolution-ary movement opposed to Roman oppression of Palestine. The Zealots are rooted in the tradition of the Pharisees but a more aggressive movement occurred after the Temple was destroyed in 66–70 CE. Until that point, they were totally devoted to the law of Moses. Again, Jesus moves outside the box by calling one who is steeped in Pharisaic tradition to work alongside a toll collector.

Finally, we meet Judas, who is listed last among the disciples and we are told that he is the one who betrayed Jesus. Here, we have a foreshadow of Jesus' demise and the Gospel writer names names—it is Judas who will set things in motion leading to Jesus' death.

Jesus commissions the Twelve to be about his business. He authorizes and commands them to cast out demons and to heal every manner of diseases and sickness. *All* of the disciples are so authorized. So, though we know Judas to be treacherous from the very beginning of his call (his identity is wrapped up in his one act of betrayal), he *is* among those who extend the work and ministry of Jesus throughout the region. Judas casts out demons, cleanses lepers, gives sight to the blind, feeds the hungry, clothes the naked, causes deaf folks to hear, causes the lame to walk and dance and leap—Judas does these things in the name of and under the authority of Jesus. Judas is among those who witness Jesus' power, his verbal sparrings with his opponents, his times of reflection and prayer. Further, he is privy to Jesus' private sessions of conversation, table fellowship, and special teachings. So, we are puzzled at what Judas does later in the story.

Jesus' suffering and death is called the Passion story. Included are the events of his arrest, trial, and crucifixion found in the Gospels. The term "Passion" story or narrative is not found in the Bible but each Gospel gives an account of Jesus' last days on earth. It is the Passion that forms the core of Christianity—that Jesus lived, suffered, died, and was raised from the dead.

Without the Passion, we wouldn't have much of a Gospel tradition. Jesus would be merely a man who did good things but disappeared and whose movement disintegrated with his death. But the glorious Good News is that God did not let death have the final word! But, I digress—let us go back to Matthew's version of the Passion.

In Matthew, Jesus is the powerful Son of Man who knows his fate:

> When Jesus had finished saying all these things, he said to his disciples, "You know that after two days the Passover is coming, and the Son of Man will be handed over to be crucified." (MATT. 26:1–2)

Jesus has completed his teaching ministry and events take place quickly. In the context of the Passover, a time of remembering God's saving act and Moses' obedience, Jesus tells of his own suffering and death. During Passover, pilgrims from all over the region gather in Jerusalem to worship, celebrate, and praise God. Maintaining the peace is the order of the day; extra troops are dispatched to Jerusalem to quell any potential problems and to avert violence of any kind.

The opponents of Jesus have already sealed his fate but they want to avoid any riotous reaction by the masses of people who like him—see Matthew 26:3–4.

We finally see Judas again in Matthew 26:14–16:

> *Then one of the twelve, who was called Judas Iscariot, went to the chief priests and said, "What will you give me if I betray him to you?" They paid him thirty pieces of silver. And from that moment he began to look for an opportunity to betray him.*

We learned earlier (10:4) that Judas would betray Jesus; here we see how. Judas is the actor in this scene who seeks an audience with the chief priests and poses a proposition that the priests are eager to take. So eager that they pay him thirty pieces of silver for a promise of delivering Jesus to them. Matthew does not tell us why Judas strikes a deal with the chief priests. The money is not considered to be a large sum, so Judas is certainly not expecting to get rich by committing his act of betrayal. The sum is more like a tip than a payment. It is difficult to believe that Judas' motive is rooted in greed; if it is, he is no financial planner here.

The Passion narrative continues: Jesus sends the disciples out to make preparations for the Passover meal at the home of an unnamed man in Jerusalem (26:17–19). It seems that Judas is also part of the delegation that makes the Passover arrangements. Later, Jesus dines with his disciples and continues to outline his fate—read Matthew 26:20–25.

Here, we see Jesus and Judas interacting. To this point in Matthew, Judas has been in the background. There has not been, until now, any specific verbal exchange between Jesus and Judas. It is interesting to note that Jesus does not call Judas out and expose his deed. It seems as though none of the other disciples know what Judas is up to; but Jesus knows and lets Judas know that he knows. The statement, *"Surely not I . . . "* is not a reflective or contemplative question; rather it is a statement of certainty that the one speaking is not the betrayer—almost like, "Well, it certainly is not I who will betray you, is it?" The statement implies a confidence but leaves a glimmer of possibility that it could be the speaker who will betray.

Ironically, Judas makes the same statement as the other disciples but with an important difference. The others call Jesus "Lord"—a title of respect and an indicator of "insider" status. That is, the disciples disclose the sense of intimacy and connection by referring to Jesus as the Sovereign One. On the other hand, Judas calls Jesus "Rabbi"—the term that outsiders use. Judas always refers to Jesus as "Rabbi" in Matthew.

Scholars make note of the difference in titles to highlight Judas' status. In some ways, he has remained an outsider despite his call into the inner circle. Judas is the only non-Galilean disciple and may have had some feelings of insecurity about that. Judas sneaks off by himself to negotiate with the chief priests. Judas is secretive and devious despite the life he has shared with Jesus and his companions. Already knowing that he has been paid to hand Jesus over, Judas continues his charade. He pretends to be loyal while waiting for an opportunity to betray Jesus.

Yet despite Judas' deceit, Jesus is well aware of what will take place. In this matter, Matthew makes it clear that Jesus is no tragic victim. Instead, Jesus predicts his betrayal, names his betrayer, and sets the frame for the betrayal—no one takes his life, Jesus gives it up, in his own time and his own way.

What makes Judas' statement of loyalty all the more disappointing is the context within which he speaks. He is one at the table with Jesus. Table fellowship is a place of intimacy, friendship, and hospitality. The one who shares the bowl with Jesus is the betrayer. Matthew makes it clear that Jesus' demise is inevitable; but of his betrayer, *"It would have been better for that one not to have been born . . . "* Perhaps, these are the words that will echo in Judas' ears and heart later in the narrative.

After instituting communion, Jesus leads the disciples to the Mount of Olives where he announces that all the disciples will abandon him. The disciples will "fall away" (NIV) or "become deserters" (NRSV)—*skandalismós*—they will be filled with terror and flee in fear. In their panic, they will forget their earlier protests against betraying Jesus. He knows this and lets them know that he knows. Again, they protest with Peter being the most verbal about his loyalty (Matt. 26:32–35).

Then, Jesus goes with the disciples to Gethsemane to pray. He takes Peter, James, and John off for special prayer. There are three tragicomedic moments contrasting Jesus' great distress and the three disciples' incapacity to stay awake to pray with him (Matt. 26:37-46). On the third time, Jesus indicates that his hour has arrived:

> Then [Jesus] came to the disciples and said to them, "Are you still sleeping and taking your rest? See, the hour is at hand, and the Son of Man is betrayed into the hands of sinners. Get up, let us be going. See, my betrayer is at hand."
> (MATT. 26:45–46)

Suddenly, Judas reappears. It is not clear when he left the group. There were several opportunities: after the singing of the hymn following communion (26:30); after leaving the Mount of Olives (26:36); or, after Jesus took Peter, James, and John off to the side to pray (26:37). All we know, for sure, is that Judas left the group to let the chief priests know where Jesus was. Read Matthew 26:47–56.

Curiously, Judas is referred to, not as the betrayer, but as one of the Twelve. This highlights how truly separated and alienated Judas is from Jesus and his fellow disciples. While the others are with Jesus (albeit they are asleep and disengaged), Judas is off doing his own thing. Instead of being in the fold, Judas is outside the circle working deeds of destruction. And the story gets worse . . .

A large crowd armed with weapons accompanies Judas. He walks up to Jesus and greets him with a kiss. Again, Judas uses the outsider's greeting of "Rabbi." Jesus does not resist him and, in essence, encourages Judas in his treachery: *Jesus said to him, "Friend, do what you are here to do"* (Matt. 26:50a). The interaction between Jesus and Judas again is terse and highlights the dramatic tension between the two.

Judas has the option to change his mind against handing Jesus over to the authorities. He fails each time and stays the course. Likewise, Jesus can stop the action or change its course; he, too, lets the events play out. Both men do what they must do to move the story along.

Judas' kiss heightens the drama. The words translated kiss/kissed *(phileo, kataphileo)* are rooted in a Greek word that means treating someone as if s/he is related and is one Greek word for love. The kiss is an act of affection but does not carry sexual implications; it is like the love between parents and children, friends, and such. Kisses convey respect and honor. As a sign of respect, kisses are usually placed on the hands or feet but also can be placed on the cheeks, forehead, eyes and shoulders. Here, when we are told that Judas will kiss Jesus, *phileo* is used. However, when he actually kisses Jesus, *kataphileo* is used and implies that Judas kisses Jesus fervently and more than once. His kiss(es) seems to be one of recognition and part of his greeting. After the kiss, Judas disappears until chapter 27. Things move quickly now—Jesus is arrested and the disciples—all of them—desert him and run away, just as Jesus predicted. Further, Jesus again is shown in control of the action:

> "... Do you think that I cannot appeal to my Father, and he will at once send me more than twelve legions of angels? But how then would the scriptures be fulfilled, which say it must happen in this way?" (MATT. 26:53–54)

Jesus stands before Caiaphas, the high priest, and is sent to Pilate. Before Jesus is condemned and sentenced to die, Matthew interjects a parting word about Judas: read Matthew 27:3–10.

There are some interesting features in the passage:

➤ Matthew is the only Gospel that talks about Judas after Jesus is arrested in Gethsemane;

> ➤ Matthew says that Judas repented, *metamelomai,* meaning to have feelings of remorse or regret. The word does not carry the Hebrew connotation of turning around or a total change of heart and mind. Judas is sorry but does not experience genuine, deep repentance for his act of betrayal, which would be signaled by a different orientation to life and relationship;

> ➤ Judas goes to the Temple to meet with the chief priests when the action around Jesus is at Caiaphas' home;

> ➤ Matthew begins to flesh out Judas' character.

Judas, who is now again referred to as the "betrayer," realizes his mistake and repents. Only at this point does Judas have a change of heart. He tries to make things right: he is contrite; takes back the money; and confesses his "sin" in betraying innocent blood. It is not clear why Judas seeks absolution from the very men who paid him to hand Jesus over to them. Instead of pleading his case to Jesus, Judas seeks forgiveness from those whose only concern is detaining and killing Jesus. What is more, now that they have Jesus, the chief priests and elders could care less about Judas and his guilty conscience:

> [Judas] said, "I have sinned by betraying innocent blood." But they said, "What is that to us? See to it yourself." (MATT. 27:4B)

Judas is frustrated and, no doubt, disgusted with himself. He throws the thirty pieces of silver down and goes out to hang himself. Judas takes actions into his own hands and makes a fateful decision.

Judas remains on the outside. He never reunites with the other disciples. He never sees or speaks to Jesus again. Matthew does not give us reasons why Judas betrayed Jesus. Matthew softens our judgment of Judas in that we see a fallen, remorseful figure who realizes, too late, that he could have made a different choice. Totally lost in hopelessness and despair, Judas commits suicide and that is where his story ends.

Matthew uses Mark as a source for his Gospel. Mark treats Judas in ways similar to Matthew. In Mark, Judas is listed among the Twelve (3:14–19). Here, the list begins with Simon (Peter) and ends with

Judas, "the one who betrayed" Jesus. The origin of "Iscariot" continues to be debated among scholars. Some think the name indicates that Judas is a man (Hebrew: *ish*) from the southern town, Kerioth. Others suggest that the name is derived from the Greek *sikarios*, which means "assassin." Still others suggest that Judas is a man *(ish)* from Issachar. All we know for certain is that Judas is from Judea in the south.

We meet Judas next in Mark 14:10–11 where he conspires with the chief priests to capture Jesus. Notice that Judas is referred to as "one of the twelve." In contrast to Matthew's version, in Mark's version the chief priests (note the absence of the elders found in Matthew) are delighted at the prospect of having Jesus handed over to them. Here, they promise an undisclosed sum of money but do not pay him. Judas waits for an opportunity to carry out his deed.

Mark does not elaborate on Jesus' passion prediction that one of the Twelve will hand him over. There is no specific exchange between Jesus and Judas (Mark 14:17–21). After the time in Gethsemane, Jesus indicates that the time of his betrayal is at hand (14:41–42).

Mark tells us about the deal Judas strikes with those from the chief priests, scribes (absent in Matthew), and the elders:

> *Now the betrayer had given them a sign, saying, "The one I will kiss is the man; arrest him and lead him away under guard." (*MARK 14:44)

With his kiss and outsider's greeting to Jesus ("Rabbi"), Judas disappears from Mark's Gospel. Mark does not tell us anything that would help us understand Judas' actions.

In Luke's Gospel, we first meet Judas in 6:12–16 where the Twelve are named. Luke relies on Mark but differs in several ways:

- ➤ In Luke, Jesus calls his disciples and chooses twelve. This opens the possibility that there were many disciples that might have included women among their ranks.

- ➤ In Luke, Jesus chooses twelve and names them "apostles." Apostles are those who are witnesses to Jesus' ministry—they are chosen, commissioned and accompany Jesus while he teaches and ministers. They are witnesses to the resurrection event. Jesus names the Twelve to be leaders.

➤ In Luke, there are two named Judas—Judas the son of James (perhaps the same one called Thaddeus in Matt. 10:3 and Mark 3:18) and Judas Iscariot.

Luke's list begins with Simon (Peter) and ends with Judas, "who became a traitor." We next see Judas in Luke 22 where the chief priests and scribes have decided to kill Jesus at an opportune time. They do not want to kill Jesus during the Passover festival because they fear the people will riot. Luke adds a twist to the Synoptic treatment of Judas:

> *Then Satan entered into Judas called Iscariot, who was one of the twelve . . .*
> (LUKE 22:3)

Judas takes the initiative and bargains with the chief priests (note the absence of the scribes and elders) and the temple police officers. Money is promised but not given.

Interestingly, Satan reappears in the narrative. Luke introduces Satan during Jesus' temptations (Luke 4:1–12) where we are left on an ominous note

> When the devil had finished every test, he departed from him until an opportune time. (LUKE 4:13)

It appears that the "opportune" time is at hand. Luke does not tell us Judas' motive and, in a sense, absolves him of guilt. In a way, Luke implies that Judas does not act on his own but rather acts under the influence of Satan. In Luke, Satan represents opposition to God's Realm (Kingdom). Satan is ruler of this world and works against God's efforts to establish a new world order. Thus, it is interesting to note that Satan pushes Judas to conspire with religious leaders against Jesus.

Luke has Jesus predict that his betrayer is in the midst of the disciples after the Last Supper. Read Luke 22:21–23. Jesus' demise is linked to the fulfillment of God's "plan" of human redemption. After Jesus' passion prediction that one of the inner circle will betray him, the disciples argue about who is the greatest among them. Jesus makes it clear that the greatest is the one who stays loyal to him (Luke 22:24–30). Jesus predicts Peter's failure (Luke 22:31–34). Then, Jesus goes to the Mount of Olives to pray (note that he does not go to Gethsemane or a garden) for strength and courage. Suddenly, Judas appears (Luke 22:47–48).

Luke does not include some Synoptic details: no description of the size of the crowd or their weapons; no mention of Judas' deal with the officials that included the kiss as a signal; Judas' words to his cohorts in the plot to capture Jesus. Here, Judas does not greet Jesus. As he approaches him, Jesus poses a question—*but Jesus said to him, "Judas, is it with a kiss that you are betraying the Son of Man?"* (Luke 22:48). Judas does not answer and is not heard of again in Luke's Gospel. Jesus' prediction of betrayal has happened.

John's Gospel is different from the Synoptic Gospels. The first disciples are not called away from their everyday lives. In John 1:35–42, Jesus is minding his own business until he sees two men following him; they are disciples of John the Baptist who is testifying about Jesus, whom John calls the "Lamb of God." This title takes us back to the Hebrew Bible but scholars are divided about specific references; many suggest it refers to the Suffering Servant in Second Isaiah (Isaiah 53:7). The gist of the title suggests that Jesus is the one who redeems the world and absolves its sins.

Jesus asks the men what they are looking for; they answer with a question of their own—where is Jesus staying? They address him as "Rabbi" (a term used by outsiders in the Synoptics). Both questions carry theological meaning—for, indeed, we must ask ourselves what we are looking for if we would follow Jesus. And, where Jesus stays is important; the Greek word, *menō*, indicates that if Jesus stays with God, the relationship is strong, permanent, and eternal. The first two disciples are not named; the next day, Jesus sees Philip and commands him to follow. Philip recruits Nathanael, who utters that fateful question: *Nathanael said to him, "Can anything good come out of Nazareth?"* (John 1:46). Nathanael's name is not listed in the other Gospels' lists of the Twelve. Philip indicates that Jesus is the one promised in the law and the prophets, making him a divine messenger. John adds Jesus' earthly parentage to indicate his humanity.

It is interesting to note that one of the disciples is skeptical about Jesus' identity. Nathanael wants some proof about who Jesus is (1:45–47). In this short passage, Jesus is given a number of titles:

- ➤ "Lamb of God," an image of Jesus as savior of the world;

- ➤ "Rabbi," a title of respect used by those seeking knowledge; it means "Teacher;"

- ➤ "Messiah," a title meaning "God's Anointed One;"

- ➤ "Son of God," a title recognizing that God is Jesus' true parent;

- ➤ "King of Israel," a title linking Jesus to God's chosen people and recognizing that Jesus' authority comes from God.

John's list of early disciples names Andrew first, then Simon Peter, Philip, and Nathanael. We don't meet Judas until chapter 6. The first mention of him is when Jesus "predicts" that he will be betrayed (John 6:63). Jesus elaborates and calls his betrayer a devil (see John 6:66–71).

The backdrop of our first view of Judas is the aftermath of Jesus' feeding miracle in John 6:1–15. Jesus has to deal with the disbelief of the crowd despite the miracle and then he has to deal with issues with the disciples. In John's Gospel, neither the crowd, the religious authorities, nor the disciples ever seem to get it. They are often baffled, puzzled, bewildered, and confused. Thus, Jesus engages in lengthy discourses in an effort to make himself clear and understood.

The feeding of the five thousand also serves as the background for the Eucharistic meal at 6:53–59. Jesus knows his disciples will not understand his teaching and some will not believe. Further, he expects that many will turn back and refuse to follow him; so Jesus asks the poignant question of the Twelve: *"Do you also wish to go away?"* It is here that we meet Judas:

> Jesus answered them, "Did I not choose you, the twelve? Yet one of you is a devil."
> He was speaking of Judas son of Simon Iscariot, for he, though one of the twelve,
> was going to betray him. (JOHN 6:70–71)

Only here, 6:66–67, and 20:24 does John even mention the Twelve as a collective. Neither does John include call narratives beyond 1:35–51. Judas' reputation precedes him—here in verse 70, he is called a devil to indicate his allegiance to the forces of evil rather than to God. At a time when things should be going well for Jesus, things begin to unravel. From the very beginning, his disciples have questions about Jesus' identity and mission. Constantly, they are confused and want Jesus to give them private tutoring lessons—and even in his closest ranks, there is a devil.

We next see Judas at John 12:4. The backdrop is the anointing of Jesus by a woman (see Matt. 26:1–13 and Mark 1:3–9 which connects this scene with his passion; Luke 7:36–49 is where Jesus' feet are anointed out of love and respect). John has elements of both traditions here—read John 12:1–8. Here, however, the grumbling of the disciples about the cost is elaborated on:

> But Judas Iscariot, one of his disciples (the one who was about to betray him),
> said, "Why was this perfume not sold for three hundred denarii and the money
> given to the poor?" (He said this not because he cared about the poor, but
> because he was a thief; he kept the common purse and used to steal what was
> put into it.) Jesus said, "Leave her alone. She bought it so that she might keep
> it for the day of my burial. You always have the poor with you, but you do not
> always have me." (JOHN 12:4–8)

John gives us another glimpse of Judas. He is identified as the group treasurer and labeled a thief. We can expect very little from Judas; even his motives are suspect. He is not to be trusted; yet, he is among the Twelve. Jesus challenges Judas but does not dismiss him from the inner circle. There is no place in the Gospel where Judas is held accountable for stealing from the common fund.

We next see Judas at Jesus' Last Supper with the disciples before his arrest. Jesus' hour has come and he prepares to end his earthly ministry. Sadly, Jesus knows what Judas is up to:

> *The devil had already put it into the heart of Judas son of Simon Iscariot to betray him.* (JOHN 13:2)

There is no turning back now and Jesus can only move forward to death. But he moves with an unspeakable confidence because Jesus knows that he comes from God and is returning to God.

Jesus washes the feet of his disciples as a sign of love, service, and hospitality. Yet John continues to remind us of Jesus' impending betrayal:

> *"One who has bathed does not need to wash, except for the feet, but is entirely clean. And you are clean, though not all of you." For he knew who was to betray him; for this reason he said, "Not all of you are clean."* (JOHN 13:10B–11)

Judas is "clean" but he has already separated himself from the group because of the devil's influence.

The drama continues as Jesus explains the significance of the foot washing. And his heart is heavy because he does not have unanimous support from the Twelve and he quotes Psalm 41:9—*I am not speaking of all of you; I know whom I have chosen. But it is to fulfill the scripture, 'The one who ate my bread has lifted his heel against me'* (John 13:18). Still, Jesus remains in control of his destiny. No one takes his life; Jesus freely gives it. He wants the disciples to know that his death is part of a larger plan under the control of God.

Jesus is back at supper with the disciples after the foot washing. Events will move quickly now—read John 13:21–30. This episode is packed with drama and suspense. Jesus and Judas know what the other disciples do not: that it is time for Jesus to die. Jesus announces his betrayal and identifies the one who will hand him over, but the other disciples are uncertain about who it is. And perhaps, we, too, should be uncertain. Is Judas the betrayer or is Satan? What we know is that the struggle is bigger than Judas. The fact that the other disciples do not know the identity of the betrayer fits well with the picture of them so far in the Gospel. They know but not fully. Jesus does not try to stop Judas but instead tells him to go quickly about his task, which he does. Ominously, we are told, *". . . it was night."*

John's Gospel is filled with contrasts: flesh and spirit; believers and nonbelievers; good and evil; and light and darkness. Judas leaves the light of the world and ventures into the night; this, my friends, is not a good sign for Judas or Jesus. But we are reminded that Jesus is in control of the events leading up to his arrest.

After a lengthy set of teachings and his parting discourse, Jesus and his disciples move to an undisclosed garden where Jesus often met with them. Judas knows the place and brings the authorities with him. Only John counts Roman and Jewish soldiers among those who come to arrest Jesus. In the Synoptics, Judas is the active one who greets and/or kisses. Here, Judas stands mute, clearly on the side of Jesus' opponents—the Roman soldiers, chief priests, and Pharisees (note the absence of the elders). Jesus is the actor here—he asks questions and identifies himself. The scene is the best of high drama and suspense and intrigue. At any moment, anything can happen. But Jesus is in total control. Jesus' prediction of betrayal is fulfilled and Judas disappears from the narrative. And so we are left to explain Judas' story.

There are few options and even those are unsatisfactory. We would feel better if we could come up with a list of reasons about why Judas hands Jesus over to the authorities. The Gospel writers don't give ulterior motives for his actions. Sadly, Judas is identified by his single act of treachery and we never have even a glimpse of who he might be.

We know nothing of his background or his family. All we can presume is that one day, in the normal course of his life, he encountered Jesus of Nazareth who invited him to join a reform movement rooted in God's vision and intention for creation. We can only presume that

Judas jumped in with both feet and accepted the joys and costs of discipleship. We can only surmise that Judas worked his own miracles and wonders and that he completed his acts of service and ministry just like the other disciples.

His motives could not easily have been greed—for thirty pieces of silver were barely a day's wages. If that was the best bargain he could strike, he wasn't very skilled as a treasurer. Some commentators suggest that Judas was jealous of Jesus; some say that Judas was trying to usher in God's Realm ahead of schedule. Still others suggest that he didn't think Jesus would actually be arrested and tried and crucified. But none of these explanations is helpful in the long run.

The inclusion of Satan into the passion narrative is even more disturbing for me. If Judas falls under the influence of Satan, that makes him a mere pawn in the cosmic drama. Is Satan a force or being who takes over people against their wills? Is free will real or an illusion? Do people have real choices or are we subject to the whims of unseen powers? There are times when we seem helpless to chart our own course. My own call to the ministry seemed out of my control. My efforts to resist the call resulted in physical and emotional turmoil; I did not feel a sense of peace until I surrendered and entered seminary. Did I have a real choice or was God "forcing" me into a direction I didn't want at that time?

Jesus is said to have known his destiny and he met it willingly. The conflict between Jesus and the forces that would destroy him too closely mirror our own internal, spiritual conflicts.

Judas' story, taken as a collective from the Synoptics and John, highlights several things:

➤ That Judas' inclination toward betrayal is a human trait. All of us walk a thin line between loyalty and betrayal. None of us are exempt from those moments when we might side against Jesus. In little choices and big decisions, we don't know which way we will decide.

➤ That Jesus is keenly aware of who he is and what his purpose is. Jesus does not get sidetracked or distracted from fulfilling his purpose. That he would rather live than die makes him human. That he marched right into his death makes him heroic. That God raised him from death makes him divine.

➤ That regardless of human agency, God finds a way to move things forward. We cannot know how salvation would have evolved had Judas decided not to betray Jesus. But we know that the results would have been the same—God will not leave us alone. God will find a way to stay connected to us humans. Whatever is in the hearts of humans, God is able to redeem it for God's purposes. In this way, we can declare with Joseph when he speaks a word of forgiveness to his brothers: *"Even though you intended to do harm to me, God intended it for good . . . "* (GENESIS 50:20)

➤ That God took the worst of human treachery and turned it into a triumph for God's own glory. The cross was a symbol of shame, resignation, and despair. If death had had the final word, then God and the forces of good would have been defeated and Jesus would have duped us. The despair of Good Friday, however, gave way to the hope of Easter Sunday—Jesus is alive and thanks be to God!

We cannot stand for long in judgment and condemnation of Judas. If we do, we also indict ourselves, for a bit of Judas is alive in each of us. Judas had the potential to be great among the disciples and apostles. He chose a path that led him away from Jesus rather than closer to him. The great traditions of the faith were not enough to keep Judas on the side of Jesus.

Judas is not able to speak for himself and we cannot leave him as the unforgiven and unforgivable traitor—Judas, bad boy that he may be, is more like us than we may care to consider.

REFLECTION QUESTIONS

1. Read Acts 1:16–25. How do you understand this explanation about Judas' last days?

2. Have you ever felt like an outsider? What would make you feel welcome in a situation?

3. Is it easy or difficult for you to forgive? What would be unforgivable for you?

4. Judas' character is maligned in all four Gospels. Yet he exercises initiative, has drive, is patient—name some other positive qualities of Judas. Explain your choices.

5. It has been suggested that Judas, as the only non-Galilean disciple, always felt uncomfortable and left out among the other eleven disciples. What makes you feel wanted? What can you do to make others feel welcomed and needed?

6. The fear of informants was a real challenge in Jesus' day and during the early days of the church. How should traitors be handled? What should the church do about traitors?

7. Have you ever been betrayed? Have you ever betrayed someone? Explain.

8. Does God micro-manage our lives? Do you believe in human free will? Explain. Are there examples in your life that contradict your belief?

9. Judas is a symbol of the tension between fellowship and betrayal. How do you develop trust with others?

10. In what ways do you betray Jesus? Explain.

11. The other disciples are guilty of personal weaknesses and ambitions, lack of faith and failure to understand Jesus and his mission. Why do you think they are not held accountable for their acts of disloyalty? Why are they forgiven and not also Judas?

12. If Judas' role is to move Jesus toward the cross so he could be raised and glorified by God, then should Judas be considered a heroic martyr? Why or why not?

13. Do you have a sense of destiny? What is it? What role does God play in your movement toward your life's purpose?

14. Judas tries to undo his deed by appealing to the chief priests and returning the money. Have you ever wished you could undo a decision and start over? Explain.

15. Judas never goes back to the community of the disciples. He dies in despair. What can the church do to (re)claim those who stand outside the church?

16. There are two suicides by hanging in the Bible (see 2 Samuel 17:23). What can the church do to prevent suicides? How can the church comfort family and friends of those who commit suicide?

17. What do you imagine Judas gave up to follow Jesus? What do you think he was looking for by following Jesus?

7

PONTIUS PILATE: "CAN'T WE ALL JUST GET ALONG?"

READ JOHN 18:28—19:16A

Pilate is the most powerful man in Judea at the height of Jesus' ministry and mission. His job is to maintain law and order. According to historians, Pilate did his job and did it well. What would he do when confronted by Jewish leaders to execute a little known carpenter from Nazareth? For a man who just wanted to do his job, Pilate takes center stage for a brief but defining moment in the drama of salvation history.

Pontius Pilate was the Roman prefect in Judea during 25–36 CE. As the region's fifth governor, Pilate was in office during the ministries of John the Baptist and Jesus of Nazareth. His job was to maintain peace and to check into any situations of potential trouble. He had a military force of some 3,000 troops at his command and did not hesitate to use them. Jerusalem was a hotbed of turmoil in those days and Pilate was kept busy. As judge and executioner, Pilate's docket was often filled with cases on civil disobedience and outright rebellious violence. Historians paint quite a negative picture of him. His conflicts with the Jewish population of Jerusalem are well documented. He seemed to find new ways to offend the Jews.

Josephus, first century Jewish historian, documents numerous instances where Pilate just didn't get it or care about how he abused his Jewish subjects. One infamous incident could be called "Watergate." Pilate needed funds for his aqueduct project. He took money from the Temple treasury without permission. When the Jews protested, Pilate had his soldiers disguise themselves as Jews and join the protest demonstrations. At a pre-arranged signal, he had the soldiers attack the protesters, killing hundreds. Many more were injured in the ensuing chaos. Pilate was not above using brutal force in his attempts to control the people. In fact, it was his attack on a group of Samaritans that caused his recall from office. On his way to answer to the Emperor about his latest fiasco, the Emperor died and Pilate disappears from the pages of history.

We know little about his life before and even less about his life after his tenure in Judea. Legends abound, including that he and his wife converted to Christianity. In fact, the Coptic and Greek Orthodox churches made Pilate and his wife saints of the church. Early Christian art portrays him as a friend of the Christian movement and places him alongside the likes of Abraham and Daniel.

We have a picture of him in the Gospels, though scholars generally agree that we don't have objective portraits of him. In all of the Gospels, the blame for Jesus' crucifixion has been transferred from Pilate to either the Jews at large or the Jewish religious leaders. Mark provides the basic outline for what we see of Pilate's interaction with Jesus (Mark 15:1–15). The morning following Jesus' arrest, the Sanhedrin takes him to be handed over to Pilate. Pilate questions Jesus—*"Are you the King of the Jews?"* Jesus answers affirmatively. The chief priests cite a list of charges against Jesus who does not speak in his defense. The crowd demands that Jesus be executed. Pilate tries to change their minds but they are not to be deterred. Pilate, under pressure, releases Barabbas and sends Jesus to be flogged and crucified.

John's Gospel, however, gives us an opportunity to see Jesus interact differently with Pilate. The episode is found beginning with John 18:28. Jesus has been handed over to a detachment of soldiers and police of the chief priests and the Pharisees (18:3). Jesus stands before the highly influential and former high priest, Annas (18:13), who interrogates him about his disciples and his teachings. It is not clear whether the "disciples" refer to the Twelve or to John's Christian community. In this scene, Jesus borders on arrogance—the high priest shouldn't ask Jesus about his teachings. Ask those who heard them since Jesus taught in public places and out in the open. Annas is so outdone by his response that he sends Jesus straight to Caiaphas (18:19–24).

There is some confusion about the identity of the high priest since Annas *and* Caiaphas carried the title. Scholars suggest that Annas' influence was felt long after his tenure ended in 15 CE. It is likely that others continued to call him "high priest" because of his emeritus status and his influence over his sons, son-in-law, and grandson who succeeded him.

We are told that Annas sends Jesus to Caiaphas but John does not report a meeting. We next see Jesus at Pilate's headquarters (18:28). Now begins the drama that contains both comedic and tragic elements. Most scholars divide the episode into seven scenes, outlined below:

> ➤ SCENE ONE—READ JOHN 18:29–32: The delegation of police and religious leaders take Jesus to Pilate. They do not enter Pilate's headquarters because to do so (enter the place of a Gentile) would render them ritually unclean and unable to participate in the Passover festival. Pilate *goes out* to them to find out the charges against Jesus. If Jesus is accused of blasphemy, he should be judged and punished by the Sanhedrin. But the delegation insists that Jesus is guilty of a crime against Rome, which is a capital offense.

> ➤ SCENE TWO—READ JOHN 18:33–38A: Pilate *goes in* to question Jesus. As is his way in John's Gospel, Jesus answers a question with a question. The question sets the tone for their entire interaction because Pilate's response determines whether he will be his own person or fall under the influence and pressure of the "Jews." Pilate's answer is pointed—*"I am not a Jew, am I?"* And for the rest of the trial, Pilate will be answering that question. For John, being a "Jew" is about refusing to accept Jesus as God's Messiah. Nonbelievers are "Jews" and, most especially, those members of the religious establishment. So the staunchest Pharisee, Sadducee, chief priest, scribe, and elder are "Jews," because they fail to see what God is doing in the

person and work of Jesus. Pilate's belief or disbelief will determine whether he is, indeed, a Jew. Jesus tells him what believers already know—that his "kingdom" or realm is from God and is about God's intention for humanity and creation. Jesus' realm stands in opposition to the earthly realm that so concerns Pilate and the Jewish authorities. Both are concerned with holding on to their power, prestige, and presence rather than about doing the work of God. The truth is that God is truly doing a new thing—beginning with John the Baptist and continuing in Jesus. In fact, Jesus is the truth. So Pilate's question, *"What is truth?"* has the ring of irony. He asks *the* Truth what truth is—Pilate is proving that, to his dismay and in ways yet to be revealed, he is a "Jew."

➤ SCENE THREE—READ JOHN 18:38B–40: Pilate doesn't wait for Jesus' answer but *goes out* to talk to the Jews, states that their case is bogus and that he is willing to release to them their "King." They refuse the offer and ask for Barabbas instead. Pilate taunts the Jewish delegation by referring to Jesus as their king. All four Gospels cite the practice of releasing a prisoner at the Passover although there is no evidence of this found in sources outside the Bible. From the Synoptics (Matt. 27:15–26; Mark 15:6–15; Luke 23:18–25), we learn that Barabbas is a violent and murderous revolutionary who is guilty as charged. The "Jews" reject their "king" for a bona fide criminal—the irony here is tragic as they dig an ever-deepening hole for themselves.

➤ SCENE FOUR—READ JOHN 19:1–3: Pilate *goes in* and has Jesus flogged; the Roman soldiers taunt and abuse him. Most of us have no idea what a flogging is and thus we miss the horror of it. One is stripped of all clothing and tied to a post so that the back is exposed. One is repeatedly hit with a leather thong woven with pieces of sharp bone and/or metal. At the end of the flogging, one's back is cut to shreds—raw, bleeding, and lacerated. Floggings are often the prelude to crucifixion and sometimes the victims die from the flogging alone. The soldiers place a thorned crown on Jesus' head and dress him in the royal purple robe as they hit him in his face.

➤ Scene Five—Read John 19:4–7: Pilate *goes out* and plays the scene like a talk show host by introducing and presenting Jesus with his crown of thorns and purple robe: *Indeed, here is the man!* Pilate seems to say. *Here is your Messiah. What a pitiful sight. What can and what will this man do for you Jews with your messianic hopes. If this is what you are looking for, you are a sorry people, to be sure!* The situation is getting out of hand. It is clear that Pilate is not taking the Jewish leadership seriously here. He continues to make fun of them at Jesus' expense. He states twice that there is no case against him; this does not indicate whether Pilate thinks Jesus is innocent, only that the religious authorities have not proven their case against him beyond a shadow of doubt. The Jews immediately sentence Jesus to die—"Crucify him!" In the Synoptics, it is the crowd that calls for Jesus' death. Here, the chief priests and police shout; John wants to place the blame for Jesus' death squarely on the shoulders of the religious leadership. So rabid is their hostility against Jesus they insist that Pilate carry out their wishes—or else!

➤ Scene Six—Read John 19:8–12: Pilate *goes in* and resumes his interrogation. He had hoped that the Jews would be satisfied with the flogging and drop their charges. But they have upped the ante and Pilate begins to see that his hands might be tied in the matter. Pilate is afraid, but we don't know why. Jesus, however, is not afraid of Pilate or the authorities because he knows their power is no match for God's. Jesus indicates that these events—his betrayal, arrest, trial, and impending death—are in God's hands. Despite the injustice of it all, God somehow will make things right. The Jews have warned Pilate of his power; Jesus warns him, too. The *"one who handed [Jesus] over to [Pilate] is guilty of a greater sin"* would seem to refer to

the "Jews." They are the religious ones who profess to know
God yet they cannot see God in Jesus; their blindness continues to cast them outside the circle of God's redemptive work.
It is not clear why Pilate seeks Jesus' release; nor is it clear
how the Jews know of his intention to release Jesus. But they
threaten to charge Pilate with treason if he releases Jesus! How
the tables have turned—the man in charge is on the verge of
being charged. Pilate may feel that a report of one more infrac-
tion of his power to the Emperor will be more trouble than it
is worth. He has been held accountable for his actions in the
past, and Pilate may want to avoid yet another case against
him.

➤ SCENE SEVEN—READ JOHN 19:13–16A: Pilate *goes out* and witnesses one of the saddest scenes in Jewish history. He brings
Jesus out with him, still wearing the makeshift crown and
bloodstained purple robe, and places him on the judge's bench.
The details of the place and time lend poignancy to the scene
(it's similar to the inquiry—"where were you when you got
the news…." One will remember exactly where one was and
what one was doing). Pilate announces again, *"Here is your King."*
There is yet time for a change of heart. The leaders still have a
chance to drop the charges against Jesus and go about their
business. They have an opportunity to change the course that
leads to the cross. As time stands still for a split second, Pilate
hopes for a reprieve. But then, the voices break the silence like
thunder, *"Away with him! Away with him! Crucify him."* Pilate tries
one final time, *"Shall I crucify your King?"*

Pilate manages to ask *all* the right questions during this trial. On many
levels, Pilate symbolizes the conscience of the Jewish leaders as well as
our own. For we must reflect on what happens here and what happens
to us when we encounter Jesus: Is he the King of the Jews? I am not a
Jew, am I? What has he done? What is truth? Where is he from? What
has he to do with us?

Through the stories of the ancestors and prophets, we have heard of God's wondrous and mysterious ways. We have witnessed God's power, mercy, and commitment to liberation. We have beheld God's ongoing struggle to create a community of love, integrity, and accountability. We have wept as God's people reject and refuse God's covenant and mercy. We have sat with God's people in the shadows and silence brought on by human stubbornness and pride. We have quietly rejoiced at the preaching and teaching of John the Baptist, hoping against hope that God has relented one more time to rescue us from aimlessness and sin. We have been amazed and awed by the healings, miracles, and teachings of Jesus of Nazareth. We have hoped that he might be the one spoken about in the law and the prophets.

But what are we to think now as our gaze falls upon the silenced one whose blood trickles down his forehead? What can we believe now as we see the streaks of blood clotting under the robe reserved for kings and queens? What can we hope from the one who sits in judgment of us all? What can we expect on the eve of Passover, a time of remembering God's definitive act of freedom and community? *"Shall I crucify your King?"* Tragically, the answer then, and too often the answer today, is yes. And not just yes, but worse: *"We have no king but the emperor."*

Here is the ultimate rejection of God. But the stage was set for this moment back in the days of the judges:

> *Then all the elders of Israel gathered together and came to Samuel at Ramah, and said to him, "You are old and your sons do not follow in your ways; appoint for us, then, a king to govern us, like other nations." But the thing displeased Samuel when they said, "Give us a king to govern us." Samuel prayed to [GOD], and [GOD] said to Samuel, "Listen to the voice of the people in all that they say to you; for they have not rejected you, but they have rejected me from being king over them. Just as they have done to me, from the day I brought them up out of Egypt to this day, forsaking me and serving other gods, so also they are doing to you. Now then, listen to their voice; only—you shall solemnly warn them, and show them the ways of the king who shall reign over them." (*1 SAMUEL 8:4–9*)

In thoroughly rejecting Jesus, the "Jews" have rejected God's offer of redemption—it's like standing on the banks of the Sea of Reeds (Red Sea) and declaring, "We ain't going!" even though a path of dry land stretched before them. It's like standing at the border of the Promised Land and saying, "Not today; thanks!" even though the light is green. It's like having one foot in the grave and the other in the land of the living and saying, "I think not!" even though angels are waiting to minister to you.

So final is this rejection that there is nothing left to say. So, Pilate hands Jesus over to be crucified. And the question haunts him, "I am not a Jew, am I?" Finally, the answer for John and his community can only be—yes, my friend, you are a Jew!

The early church worked hard to redeem Pilate and his role in the salvation story. The responsibility for Jesus' crucifixion was transferred from him to the Jewish leaders in John's Gospel. We suspect that this portrait of Pilate reflects the political situation of John's community. They did not wish to further antagonize those who held their lives in the balance. Pilate joins the groups in opposition to Jesus and lets us know that the One who came to save the world, too, is judging us. At any point in the trial, Pilate could have sided with Jesus. But he was not his own person; he gave in to the pressure of others.

Pilate's comedic shuffling back and forth (going in and going out) symbolizes the ambivalence that any of us may feel in our encounters with Jesus. We go back and forth, believing in one situation and not in another. Pilate, like Judas, could be any of us—or, we could be either Pilate or Judas, depending on the circumstances. Our indecisiveness comes and goes depending on how confident we are in our own sense of power, authority, and autonomy. Our investment in the realm of this world blinds us to a bigger, deeper, wider reality—that this is God's world and God still has the whole world in God's hands. Our choices mean nothing if they are not rooted in God's new world order.

Pilate had questionable administrative and people skills. He was judged insensitive towards those over whom he ruled. He tried to be "politically correct" by listening to and giving in to the will of the

Jewish leaders. He gave them what they said they wanted. But he made a bad moral decision—he convicted to death an innocent man. In Matthew's Gospel, Pilate's wife warns him to not get involved—but there was no way he could have avoided the situation.

The advantage we have over Pilate is that we already know how the story ends. If the cross had been the end of the story, we could not stand in judgment of Pilate for his inability and unwillingness to do the right thing. The cross is only part of the story. The emblem of shame, reserved for the most violent and vile of criminals, was an opportunity for God to continue the salvation story. Even "bad boy" Pilate could not stop this story.

REFLECTION QUESTIONS

1. In the decisions we make, do we decide for or against Jesus?

2. In what ways do we continue to crucify Jesus in our thoughts, words, and deeds? Be specific.

3. Pilate is a man of power who has to make some hard choices. His is the power of personality—but who is the real powerhouse here— Pilate or Jesus or the Jews?

4. What are Pilate's strengths as a leader? Explain your answer.

5. Mrs. Pilate sends a message to her husband: *While he was sitting on the judgment seat, his wife sent word to him, "Have nothing to do with that innocent man, for today I have suffered a great deal because of a dream about him"* (Matt. 27:19). What is the importance of her message? Do you think Pilate took her message seriously? Explain.

6. Why do you think the crowd that cheered Jesus' entry into Jerusalem (Matt. 21:8–9; Mark 11:8–10; Luke 19:36–38) turned against him at the trial before Pilate (Matt. 27:24–25)?

7. We are told that when Martin L. King, Jr. had tough decisions to make, he sat in the middle of the night at his kitchen table, reading his Bible and praying. What do you do when you have a hard decision to make?

8. What kinds of leadership qualities are needed during tough times? Be specific.

9. Have you ever made a bad decision? What happened? If you could, what would you change?

10 If you could spend thirty minutes with Jesus, what would you ask him? What would Jesus ask you?

11. How do you behave when you realize you have made a mistake? Are there other ways of reacting? Name some. What support do you need to admit your mistakes?

8

ANANIAS: "WHO'S GOING TO KNOW?"

READ ACTS 4:32–5:11

The story of Ananias is a tragic story of a man who puts on a show, only to be found out. He withholds funds from a real estate deal and pretends to give all the proceeds to the common fund at Jerusalem. Peter knows Ananias is being deceitful and calls him on it. It is not clear what or who killed Ananias; he may have died from shame or guilt. But he dies because he is a cheat who tries to get away with it.

The story of Ananias is a curious and disturbing one. It is especially haunting because it appears in the midst of a narrative that describes an ideal early church community.

The Acts of the Apostles, or simply Acts, is a historical account of the early Christian movement. It covers the period from the time of Jesus' resurrection to the missionary work of Paul in Rome. The book is a continuation of Luke's Gospel of Jesus. Acts primarily focuses on the ministries of Peter and Paul. While tracing the work of the Apostles, Acts also touches on theological, social, and political issues. The founding of the Christian church does not occur in a vacuum; rather, it is born in controversy and its early life is challenged both by internal and external forces. Through these challenges, we learn something of the Apostles' characters and their faith.

The early chapters of Acts tell us about the church at Jerusalem. The church leaders have their hands full as they mediate important issues: the relationship between Judaism and Christianity; the relationship between Jewish Christians and Gentile Christians; and the relationship between the church and the Roman authorities. Many conflicts are aired and we are left with a multifaceted picture of the early church. There are deep connections among the members, yet there are potentially divisive challenges, too.

The early church itself was a miracle! Although it had been foretold, few really believed that Jesus would be raised from death. When Jesus cried out with a loud voice, *"Father, into your hands I commend my spirit . . . "* even his own disciples thought that was the end of the movement. Their leader was dead and lay in a tomb. Their hope of a restored and glorious Israel was as lifeless as the corpse that lay behind the stone at the tomb's entrance. All that they had given up to follow the Teacher from Nazareth seemed like a foolish mistake. All the miracles, wonders, signs, and healings now seemed like a cruel hoax. All the wrangling with the Pharisees, Sadducees, priests, elders, and scribes now seemed like wasted energy. So, when word came that Jesus had been raised from the dead, the disciples were incredulous—how could this be? But Jesus *had* been resurrected and he appeared to them and taught them once again. Now the work of preparing people for the Realm of God fell squarely on the shoulders of the disciples. And they were renewed for the task at hand:

> *Then [Jesus] led them out as far as Bethany, and, lifting up his hands, he blessed them. While he was blessing them, he withdrew from them and was carried up into heaven. And they worshiped him, and returned to Jerusalem with great joy; and they were continually in the temple blessing God.* (LUKE 24:50–53)

The Holy Spirit worked through the Apostles to create the church and to increase its numbers. Things moved quickly and the Apostles were admired for their boldness and conviction of faith. They were passionate in their preaching and performed great deeds of healing. A community of compassion and unity was created:

> *Awe came upon everyone, because many wonders and signs were being done by the apostles. All who believed were together and had all things in common; they would sell their possessions and goods and distribute the proceeds to all, as any*

had need. Day by day, as they spent much time together in the temple, they broke
bread at home and ate their food with glad and generous hearts, praising God
and having the goodwill of all the people. And day by day the Lord added to
their number those who were being saved. (ACTS 2:43–47)

The community already had the marks of God's coming Realm—one
for all and all for one. This was a worshipping, praying, caring community where everyone took care of each other. Class distinctions, so
prevalent in that community before Jesus' resurrection, were down-
played as the wealthier members sold their possessions and property
and added their resources to a common fund. No one did without
because everyone shared. The picture of the Jerusalem church is pro-
saic and idealistic. So, we ought not be surprised to learn that all was
not well in paradise.

Ananias and his wife, Sapphira, are members of the Jerusalem
church. He sells a parcel of property and withholds some of the proceeds. Peter accuses him of lying to the Holy Spirit. Upon hearing
these words, Ananias falls down and dies. The details of the story are
not clear—how did Peter know that Ananias had held some of the
money back? Did Ananias die because of his deed or because of the
accusation of lying to the Holy Spirit? What does lying to the Holy
Spirit mean? How does one lie to the Holy Spirit? Did Ananias die
because he was guilty or did God kill him? In other words, what was
the cause of death? Why did the author or editor of Acts include this
story? What is this story about? Let us see if we can fit together some
pieces of this puzzle.

We know that members of the Jerusalem church pooled their
resources for the good of the community:

Now the whole group of those who believed were of one heart and soul, and no
one claimed private ownership of any possessions, but everything they owned was
held in common. There was not a needy person among them, for as many as
owned lands or houses sold them and brought the proceeds of what was sold.
They laid it at the apostles' feet, and it was distributed to each as any had need.
(ACTS 4:32, 34–35)

A short description illustrating the generosity and commitment to communal living is given at the end of chapter four. Joseph, whom the Apostles renamed Barnabas, is a Levite, native of Cyprus. He sells a field and brings the proceeds to the common fund. This act of communal love is a shining example of those in the Jerusalem church. There is no selfishness and people have the common good at heart. But . . .

We are warned in the next breath that while sharing is the ideal, there is no perfection—not even in the Mother Church.

But a man named Ananias, with the consent of his wife Sapphira, sold a piece of property; with his wife's knowledge, he kept back some of the proceeds, and brought only a part and laid it at the apostles' feet. (ACTS 5:1–2)

We are not given any details of Ananias' background or life—we are not told his hometown or even who his family is. No history or information is given about him or his wife. We know he is married to Sapphira. Theirs seems to be a good marriage—he consults her on business matters; he seems to value her opinion; and he desires her consent. We do not know whether they have children. Nor do we know the extent of their wealth—they sold a piece of property, but we don't know how many pieces of property they owned. We may only presume that they were persons of some means. Ananias' act mirrors that of Barnabas with a major exception: whereas Barnabas presents all the proceeds from his transaction, Ananias holds back.

Somehow, Peter knows of Ananias' deed and calls him on it.

"Ananias," Peter asked, "why has Satan filled your heart to lie to the Holy Spirit and to keep back part of the proceeds of the land?" (ACTS 5:3)

What an indictment Peter makes. Peter cuts right to the chase and, no doubt, leaves Ananias breathless. Peter questions Ananias' motives as well as his integrity. Peter makes the issue one of theological importance by injecting Satan and the Holy Spirit into Ananias' deed. There is a lack of compassion in this episode. Peter appears confrontational and Ananias' deception is seen as theological and spiritual suicide.

Neither Ananias nor his wife Sapphira are given opportunities to repent, explain, or make restitution.

The New Testament understanding of Satan is a carryover from that in the Hebrew Bible. The name "Satan" means "adversary." In Job 1–2 and Zechariah 3:1–2, Satan is a member of God's assembly who questions the integrity of human beings. As adversary, Satan questions God's total confidence and trust in humans. Satan is not described as God's enemy nor is he the head of evil demons. Later in Judaism's development and in the New Testament, there emerges a dualism that results in the good-versus-evil dichotomy between God and Satan.

The most common name for the forces hostile to God is "Satan," which is translated "devil" in Greek. Satan and his company come to represent that which opposes God, God's people, and God's purposes. Thus, any tendencies that thwart a utopian or ideal Christian community would be attributed to the work of Satan. In this context, Satan influences people to commit sin. Ananias, according to Peter, gives in to Satan's influence to cheat and lie. Ananias is moved to hypocrisy rather than honesty. He is moved to cheat rather than care. He is moved to hold back rather than give his all.

Peter is especially disgusted because there is no reason for Ananias to do this heinous act. Ananias' land was his to do with as he chose. He was under no legal or even spiritual obligation to sell or contribute to the common fund. It might have been a nice gesture to do so, but there was no pressure from the church leaders that would lead to coercion. But if one makes the gesture, then one needs to be honest about it:

> ". . . While [the property] remained unsold, did it not remain your own? And after it was sold, were not the proceeds at your disposal? How is it that you have contrived this deed in your heart? You did not lie to us but to God!" (Acts 5:4)

Ananias needed only to act with integrity, but he did not. Ananias tries to pass the deed off as an honest act. In essence, then, Ananias cheats, not the common fund, but God.

Now when Ananias heard these words, he fell down and died. And great fear seized all who heard of it. (ACTS 5:5)

Ananias dies and we are left to wonder why and how.

The Greek word that is translated "fear" *(phobos)* implies a widespread fright that leads to awe or apprehension among those hearing of Ananias' demise. Others in the community will be very careful about how they conduct themselves now. The rhetorical effect of Ananias' death is great fear throughout the community. Of what or of whom is the community afraid here?

We are given no reasons for Ananias' deed. Ananias never speaks to explain or defend himself. He is obviously well off; why, then, does he withhold the proceeds? Commentators suggest a couple of possibilities:

➤ Ananias and Sapphira are victims of the "keeping up with the Jones' syndrome." They seek the attention of the community that sacrificial giving brings. They seek praise and recognition for an act of generosity even though their act is dishonest.

➤ Ananias and Sapphira are foils for an unstated understanding of the early church. Members are free to make choices—good, bad, or indifferent. However, the community requires its members to behave honestly and with integrity. One either chooses self or community. If one chooses community, then certain behaviors will not be tolerated, including hypocrisy, selfishness, and dishonesty. In both testaments of the Bible, earnest devotion and service to God are tantamount to the living out of the faith. God, even in the new church, requires total devotion and service.

Ananias is held accountable for a deliberate act of dishonesty. He knowingly deceives the community and sins against the power that created the community. Luke places great emphasis on the presence and power of the Holy Spirit in his works. It is the Spirit that anoints and empowers the Apostles. It is the Spirit that calls diverse people together into a new community. It is the Spirit that opens the way for people to live together.

It is suggested that Ananias' real crime is not withholding money or lying to Peter. His crime is his inability or refusal to see the church as a creative, empowered community of the Spirit. There is no place in this new church for half-hearted efforts and divided loyalties. Ananias is an active member of the community and knows better. He has no defense and perhaps it is the full realization of his deed that kills him. Ananias has forgotten that he belongs to the risen Christ, not to Satan. If the new church is going to grow, it needs honest commitment from its members. The sin of hypocrisy cannot be tolerated, so Ananias' punishment is swift and sure.

It is not clear what motivates Ananias to do what he does. Is he looking for rewards without sacrifice? Is he defying a system that does not allow him to wallow in his riches? Is he frustrated that others are sacrificing and he might lose face if he does not comply? Is he wondering whether the Apostles are being honest themselves in the handling of the common fund? Is he simply holding back some of the cash for a rainy day or for a nest egg?

At any rate, Ananais' punishment seems severe. It is difficult for us to picture a God who strikes people down. Ananias does not have an opportunity to explain or defend himself. He never utters a word. Ananias' story mirrors that of Achan (see Joshua 7:1–26). Ananias put the church's survival in jeopardy. Better one man (and one woman) perishes than the entire movement. Ananias, no doubt, understands the importance of giving—walking the streets of Jerusalem, he sees the beggars, the widows, the orphans. There is no indication that Ananias was not previously a generous man.

We have no answers to these questions. But they haunt us even today. The early Christian church was an experiment in an alternative lifestyle. The leaders of the church strove for a community with enough of everything for everyone. The experiment was tenuous from its very beginnings. We continue to struggle with striking a balance between too much and not enough. In a society where consumerism reigns supreme, how do we live so that none have too much and all have what they need? In the midst of human need, economic uncertainty, and ecological terror, we should be filled with awe and fear. And we should recognize our part in creating a just society for all of God's people and act accordingly.

REFLECTION QUESTIONS

1. What picture of Peter emerges from this episode? What characterizes his leadership in this scene?

2. Where is God in this episode? What is the role of the Holy Spirit?

3. What does this story say about the early church?

4. What can we learn about leadership from this story? Consider lying, embezzling, and other actions that mar modern leadership.

5. What positive characteristics does Ananias display?

6. What do you think is the psychological lessons for those who witnessed this episode between Peter and Ananias? What effect does this story have on modern readers and believers?

7. Have you ever tried to "keep up with the Jones'?" What happened?

8. Describe your understanding of an ideal Christian community? Have you experienced this kind of community? Explain.

9. How can congregations hold members financially accountable? Be specific.

10. What kind of leadership is needed to guide Christian communities so that they reflect God's values?

11. What values guide your choices about material wealth and goods?

12. If Ananias and Sapphira are struck dead for merely withholding money, does the punishment fit the crime? Explain your answer.

Suggestions for Teaching and Preaching

Teaching

Bad Boys of the New Testament is designed to stimulate your curiosity and to send you on a path to further study. There are many "bad boys" not included here. I don't even mention Paul, whose life takes a dramatic turn on a Damascus road. I have not given space to Peter's story (except his role in Ananias' demise), whose impulsiveness is a lesson for us all about what not to do. Nor do I speak of Thomas, who wanted solid physical proof that Jesus was alive after the crucifixion. There is no shortage of "bad boys" in the Bible!

The Bible contains some of the most interesting and memorable stories found in all of literature. We are so familiar with these stories that we "know" things that are not even in the texts themselves. Now that we have had the opportunity to explore the stories and lives of selected biblical men, how do we go about the task of preaching and teaching about them? How do we move beyond the entertainment value and object lessons of these tales? Are there ways we can move beyond the superficial and stereotypical to explore their deeper meanings and lessons for us today? While many of the "bad boys" symbolize the "big personalities" that we may want to pattern ourselves after, they leave much to be desired as role models. How do we recognize their human frailties and flaws without demonizing them? All of their stories have something to teach us—about valor, courage, creativity, faithfulness, obedience, and love, as well as about egotism, selfishness, fear, deception, doubt, and despair.

The aims of the units are to make the stories accessible, fun, and meaningful. The following teaching ideas can be interchanged among the stories and should be attempted after studying the appropriate unit in the book. The exercises are designed to answer the following questions:

1. Who are the "characters" in the story?

2. What is the action of the story?

3. What is the challenge presented in the story?

4. Who speaks and who is silent? What do these actions mean?

5. What do we feel and think as we enact the story?

6. How is the challenge resolved?

7. What can we learn from the story?

I hope that these stories will inspire, encourage, and challenge us. How do we move beyond the "nice stories" we share in church school classes and object lesson sermons? How do we use these stories to delve deeper into who we are as children of God and disciples of Christ? How can these stories deepen our commitment to serve God and humanity in healthy ways? What can we glean from these stories that will help us along our journeys?

Many of our churches follow the Revised Common Lectionary. A lectionary is a set selection of scripture readings from the Bible. The readings are used in church services and follow the church year. The Revised Common Lectionary follows a three-year cycle (Year A, Year B, and Year C) beginning with the first Sunday in Advent. This lectionary has been endorsed by a number of church bodies throughout the world. Over a three-year period, the lectionary allows people to hear and learn from most of the New Testament, especially the Gospels and Letters, and various sections of the Hebrew Bible, including the Psalms. Typically, the lectionary will list the name of the biblical book, chapter, and verses. The lectionary readings for each Sunday generally include a reading from the Hebrew Bible, a Psalm, a selection from one of the Letters and a reading from one of the Gospels. Occasionally, there are alternative or optional readings, which provide a choice of scripture for that Sunday. Scriptures are grouped together to highlight a theme or to emphasize some aspect of Christian life (for example, Advent, Lent, Easter, Pentecost, etc.). The lectionary makes it possible for churches around the world, regardless of denominational affiliation or geography, to hear and read the same scriptures during worship and study times.

While the lectionary is an invaluable tool for church life, it sometimes makes the task of dealing with the "bad boys" more difficult. The lectionary readings do not include some of these stories or do not highlight the seedier aspects of these stories. So we have to work harder to make the stories of the "bad boys" available to our congregations. It is not surprising that many people do not know who the Pharisees are except in superficial and negative ways.

Teaching from the New Testament has its challenges. We often want to get past the hard stuff in order to celebrate the Christ event. We want to bask in God's love and focus solely on Jesus who brings God's grace and forgiveness rather than God's judgment.

We, however, cannot fully understand Jesus unless we understand the Hebrew Bible. We must remember that Jesus was a Jew, not a Christian. Jesus' worldview was shaped by the context and perspective found in the Hebrew Bible. We cannot understand how Jesus is the Messiah unless we understand how and why people looked for a sign of God's presence in the days of John the Baptist and Jesus. We cannot fully understand who this God is whom Jesus calls "Abba" ("Father"), without some sense of what this God has meant to Jesus' ancestors. The Hebrew Bible is our first story—in it we learn about the God who claimed Jesus and claims us in spite of ourselves. The Bible stands as a testimony and witness to what God is up to in the world and among us. Even more, the stories have the power to transform our lives because they reflect our human nature and God's desire not to leave us to our own resources. In the midst of all that we do, God is with us to save and redeem. Through the stories of the Bible, we learn about our own journeys of faith. We learn how to navigate the trail that leads to wholeness. We learn how to rely upon God, the source of life itself. We learn how to walk with Jesus, the author and finisher of our faith. We learn how to be fully human and fully the children of God. We are fortunate to have these stories—in their beauty and in their rawness—to show us the way to God and to wholeness!

PREACHING

Preachers have a unique opportunity to make God's story available and accessible to those who hear us. Effective preaching requires us to study, reflect, and to hone our speaking skills. Each preacher brings her or his own methods of sermon development and I encourage you to do what works for you. However, every preacher should start with the text by reading it! It helps to read the text in Greek, if you have those skills. Otherwise, use a good, reliable translation; I prefer the New Revised Standard Version (NRSV). However, I always consult more than one translation and version—paying attention to differences in wording, ordering, punctuation, etc. Then, I ask a series of questions of the text. These include:

- ➤ What is the text saying? What are the details of the story?

- ➤ Who are the participants in the story? What is said about the participants—what can we know about them?

- ➤ Who speaks and what does s/he say?

- ➤ Who is silent? Why?

- ➤ What is the setting that has given rise to this particular text?

- ➤ What is happening in the text? Who acts and what does s/he do? What are the issues involved? How are the issues resolved?

- ➤ Who reacts in the text? How? Why?

- ➤ What happens before and after this particular text? How does this text fit into the larger text?

- ➤ Are there any other biblical texts that relate to this particular text? Where? Under what circumstances are there connections?

➤ What senses (sight, sound, smell, taste, etc.) are aroused by the text?

➤ What emotions are evoked?

➤ How can we connect to the text today?

➤ What is God doing in the text? Why? To what end does God act?

➤ What is believable in the text? What raises doubt?

➤ Who in the Bible will disagree with this particular text? What would s/he say instead?

➤ Who in the church will disagree with this text? What would s/he say instead?

➤ How does this text fit into God's wider purposes for creation and humanity?

➤ What does the text say about our lives and world today?

➤ What does the text call us to be or to do? What prevents us from fulfilling the text's call? What will happen if we fail to heed the text's call? What will happen if we fulfill the text's call?

These and other questions are asked before any other sources are consulted! This method helps the preacher to see the text before her/his opinions are colored by the opinions of others. Only after wrestling with questions like these is the preacher ready to move on to study aids. Now the preacher is ready to let the sermon unfold. In the end, the aim of preaching is to bring a word of Good News to God's people—a word that is accurate, fresh, informed and interesting.

I hope that the reflection questions for each unit serve to stimulate some thinking about how these stories can be used in the church. I am sure that you have some creative ways of preaching and teaching these biblical "bad boys." I offer the following as possibilities for making these stories part of your church's life and mission. Please note that I offer only suggestions for sermons, not sermon outlines. I hope these will spark your imagination and unlock the stories so that they can bless us.

Teaching Ideas

Elder Brother

a. Imagine a talk show episode on the order of Larry King Live or Dr. Phil. The host is interviewing the unnamed mother of the son in the Prodigal Son parable. As the host, generate a set of questions you will pose to the mother. As the mother, think through a basic framework out of which you will respond to the host.

b. This is a session with a psychiatrist (or pastoral counselor) like Dr. Joyce Brothers who is counseling the two brothers. Remember that we do not see them interact in the parable. If you are the doctor, generate a set of questions that will get the brothers to begin reconciliation and kinship. If you are the younger brother, think through a basic framework out of which you will respond; remember that you are the son who asked for an early inheritance and then left home. If you are the elder brother, think through a basic framework out of which you will respond; remember, you are the son who stayed home and is now resentful that your brother has returned home to a celebration.

c. Rewrite the parable; this time, imagine that the younger son sees his elder brother first. Construct their conversation and the action that follows.

In all the scenarios, think about the action of the parable, as well as the emotions generated by and embedded in it. You may consider other biblical episodes to assist in your thinking; i.e., Jacob and Esau; Joseph and his brothers; there may be others.

Accusers of Woman Caught in Adultery

a. Imagine a grand jury where the jury needs to decide whether the accusers should stand trial for slander and defamation of character. Create speaking parts for: the judge, the jurors, the defense team, the prosecution team, and witnesses. Decide whether the accusers are guilty or innocent.

b. Imagine the woman has returned home to a waiting family. Create scenarios where she interacts with: her parents; her husband; her children; her best friend.

c. Jesus is writing a book about his encounters with the accusers. He is on a talk show and the host asks him what really happened. Prepare a five-minute presentation where Jesus presents his version of the story. A caller phones in to the show with another version—prepare a five-minute rebuttal to Jesus' story.

THE PHARISEES

a. Imagine a conference hall where debates are held. Tonight, the debate is between Jesus and a leading representative of the Pharisees. Designate a person to serve as moderator whose job is to make sure that each "candidate" has equal time to respond to questions from the audience. Other "characters" should include: Jesus, who makes a statement about his platform (what he believes, why he believes what he does, and what he hopes will happen as a result of his work); a Pharisee, who also makes a statement about her/his platform; audience members, who ask provocative and searching questions of the two. At the end of the debate, the audience will vote for a winner and state why that person won.

b. Prepare a church school lesson from the perspective of the Pharisees; emphasize doing the right thing on a particular matter—food, ritual, fasting, keeping Sabbath, etc.

JUDAS

a. Imagine that Jesus is hanging on the cross. He has uttered his first word, *"Father, forgive them…"* And his eyes fall on Judas who is on the edge of the crowd. Compose a word from Jesus just for Judas; compose a word from Jesus just for you.

b. Imagine the disciples in the Upper Room after the crucifixion. The disciples are bereft, dazed, confused, and fearful. They are wallowing in their grief and are so numb that they have not yet thought about the future. As they sit and stare at nothing in particular, with tears and cries of grief their only activity, they hear a knock at the door. Tentatively, Peter answers the door to find Judas standing there. How would each disciple react to him? How do the women react to him? Is there a word of welcome? Of forgiveness?

c. Explore the Internet for other ways to teach the story. For example, visit http://dlampel.com for a devotional one-act play about Judas.

d. Create a funeral service for Judas. In the program include: songs, prayers, eulogy, obituary, statements by family and friends; and a short homily, meditation, or sermon.

PONTIUS PILATE

a. Pilate has reached Rome and is preparing to meet Tiberius. Have Pilate prepare and rehearse his opening speech to the Emperor about the "Jesus thing." Develop a set of questions for Tiberius to use in his investigation.

b. Imagine that Pilate is writing a letter to Mary, the mother of Jesus, about the events leading up to her son's execution. What does the letter say? Write a response letter from Mary to Pilate.

c. Pilate has been asked by the leading authorities on leadership issues to keynote their annual banquet. Prepare Pilate's twenty-minute speech. Designate someone (or a team) to respond to Pilate's speech.

d. Imagine a long bus ride from Jerusalem to Nazareth. Sitting next to each other is Pilate's wife and Mary, the mother of Jesus. Create a conversation between the two.

ANANIAS

a. Rather than die on the spot, Ananias is arrested for fraud. Create a trial scene with the following characters: judge, jury, defense team, prosecution team, witnesses, and Ananias. Develop questions for the witnesses, opening and closing arguments from the lawyers. Have Ananias testify in his own defense and prepare a short statement about why he did what he did and what he had hoped to gain from his actions.

b. Ananias is the new vice president for land acquisitions for an urban planning firm. It's his first day on the job—what does Ananias say to his new team? Prepare a fifteen-minute motivational speech

PREACHING IDEAS

ELDER BROTHER

There are a number of themes in this familiar parable. Many sermons have been preached on it; common themes include: lost and found, love, repentance, forgiveness, celebration, and possibility of a second chance. Some other themes for preaching might include:

➤ The lack of adventure that the Elder Brother feels: His life has taken on a sameness, a routineness that causes him to forget how blessed he is. He takes his life for granted and feels that he has sacrificed so much, with nothing to show for it. Focus on the small things that make up our lives—the big dramatic moments may be remembered more vividly, but everyday blessings are what really count.

➤ The sense of "otherness" the Elder Brother feels: We have all felt out of place, neglected, ignored at some point in our lives. Describe those feelings and suggest how Jesus responds to our feelings of alienation.

➤ The sense of journey that life—especially the Christian life—has taken you through: Describe the journey—what are the sights, sounds, smells; what can cause detours, delays, and distractions; how do accidents and near accidents fit into the larger picture of life? How does the Christian life give us direction and focus?

➤ The kinds of things that create distance between and among people: When the Younger Brother leaves home, he places geographic distance alongside the emotional distance that allowed him to seek his inheritance early. Describe the emotional distance that the Elder Brother feels—he never addresses his father as "Father" nor his sibling as "Brother." In fact, the brothers never interact with each other at all. What can bridge distances of all types—between persons and within oneself?

The Accusers

This story holds the potential for well-meaning Christians to cast stones at the accusers—as if we would pass the test of compassion. The focus of most sermons usually centers on the exchange between Jesus and the accusers; the woman is usually left out. Some possible themes for sermons include:

➤ The woman has a second chance and we presume she takes it; what does it mean to have a second chance?

➤ The accusers walk away shamed into silence; what does it mean to repent? To judge with mercy? To care for and about people rather than about being right?

➤ The importance of forgiveness; how do we respond to forgiveness and grace?

The Pharisees

The transmission of the faith is crucial for the long-term life and health of the church and religious traditions. How do we pass our traditions on to future generations so that the traditions remain life-giving rather than oppressive? Some sermon themes include:

➤ Coupling stories about Pharisees with the Hebrew Bible's notion to remember and pass the faith to our children;

➤ When can we know if it's time to reform or change an outmoded tradition? When is change good and when is it not good? How can we know?

➤ The importance of being clear about one's identity and beliefs without being closed-minded and dogmatic;

➤ Why do we come to church? What else has a hold on us?

➤ What are some spiritual disciplines that will help people of faith today? A sermon series could be developed to address what the Bible says about: prayer, fasting, study, retreat, silence, etc.

➤ What is the relevance and application of the Ten Commandments today?

JUDAS

Too much of the church's preaching has been self-righteous and judgmental concerning Judas. But Judas was someone's son, brother, uncle, and husband. Pointedly, although we don't know many facts about his life, he was a human being. Jesus saw something in Judas that moved him to include Judas in the inner circle of disciples. Also, we must not be quick to harshly judge Judas because we may only be one decision away from betraying Jesus ourselves. Possible sermon themes include:

➤ The importance of mercy and compassion when dealing with people;

➤ The importance of outreach ministries to those who stand on the edges of our churches, communities, and world;

➤ Jesus exercises great diversity in calling the disciples—toll collector, Zealot, a Judean. How can that commitment to diversity be lived out in our churches and communities?

➤ The importance of table fellowship and hospitality—how does this relate to how we operate our churches?

➤ The role of ambivalence in our spiritual and secular lives—what can help us be more focused?

PILATE

This story highlights what can happen when church and state collude.

➤ What should be the role of each in society? Pilate was just trying to do his job, but got caught in a web of intrigue not of his making.

➤ In what ways can church and state critique each other so that we can move closer to God's vision for humanity of love, justice, mercy, and abundance?

➤ What kinds of leadership do we need in the world today? What helps or hinders that kind of leadership? What can we learn from Jesus that will help?

➤ What kinds of partnerships should we form to achieve our goals? What makes some partnerships good and others bad? What are the advantages of collaboration?

➤ Develop a dialogical sermon that eavesdrops on a conversation between Pilate's wife and Mary, the mother of Jesus.

ANANIAS

This is a difficult text to preach from without lapsing into self-righteous judgment about Ananias. The early church, however, tried to model a lifestyle within God's Realm where everyone was cared for; class distinctions were wiped away; and people lived in true community—a vision of creation that includes abundance, calls for repentance by some, and more agency by others. Sermons can be developed around the following themes:

➤ Sharing and/or withholding material and spiritual resources;

➤ The "right" use of material goods;

➤ Stewardship of time, treasure, and talents; the spiritual discipline of tithing;

➤ Seeking opportunities to serve—creating ministries of justice and compassion;

➤ Developing practical, hands-on, real life ministries to serve the less fortunate in our communities and the world;

➤ The importance of developing relationships with those whom we are called to serve—not just giving things, but also giving of ourselves.

A Final Word

I hope you have enjoyed and been challenged by *Bad Boys of the New Testament*. This book is not intended to bash these personalities in the Bible. Rather, it is intended to make them more accessible to us—so that we may learn from them, both what to do and what to avoid as we journey towards wholeness. The interactions between these bad boys and Jesus may open more questions than they answer. As we watch them plot and scheme and engage in verbal sparrings with Jesus, we sometimes feel that perhaps Jesus is the real "bad boy" here. Certainly Jesus has a different way of being in his world. He makes us stop and think about things we take for granted. The bottom line is that we cannot encounter Jesus and remain the same—somehow, he changes us and makes us better. He reminds us that we live in communities and are accountable to each other and to God.

The stories of the Bible have the power to change our lives and to give us the resources for good lives. By exploring the depths of our scripture, we gain the tools and resources needed to meet life's challenges with poise and confidence. Jesus states clearly that his purpose was not to do away with that which gave birth to two world religions; his purpose was to fulfill the law and prophets. We stand in the legacy of spiritual giants—women and men—whom I have called "bad girls and boys." I hope we have learned that they are women and men like us—flawed with the potential for divinity.

My mission is to make the Bible a lively yet challenging resource for your faith development and journey. There is no more exciting book than this witness to God's dealings with God's people. I suspect that your creativity is stimulated through these studies. I would love to hear from you about what you are learning, as well as hear questions that may be lingering from your study.

Please be in touch and let me know what you think about this book, as well as others I have written. Please let me hear from you often by visiting my website at www.barbarajessex.com.

My prayer is that you will hold these bad boys close and see in them the potential that God saw and that God continues to see in us. Travel mercies to you!

Resources Used and For Further Study

Achtemeier, Paul J. (General Editor), *Harper's Bible Dictionary*. San Francisco: Harper & Row, Publishers, 1985.

Aland, Kurt, Matthew Black, Carlo M. Martini, Bruce M. Metzger, and Allen Wikgren (Eds.) in cooperation with the Institute for New Testament Textual Research, Munster/Westphalia, *The Greek New Testament*, Third Edition. New York: American Bible Society, 1975.

Allen, Ronald J., *Preaching Luke-Acts*. St. Louis: Chalice Press, 2000.

Alling, Roger, and David J. Schlafer, *Preaching Through the Year of Luke: Sermons That Work*. Harrisburg, PA: Morehouse Publishing, 2000.

Anderson, Bernhard W., *The Unfolding Drama of the Bible* (Third Edition). Philadelphia: Fortress Press, 1988.

Barclay, William, *The Master's Men: Character Sketches of the Disciples*. Nashville: Abingdon, 1959.

Biblical Archaeology Review, www.biblicalarchaeology.org.

Bible Review, www.biblereview.org.

Bond, Helen K., *Pontius Pilate in History and Interpretation*. New York: Cambridge University Press, 1998.

Boring, M. Eugene, "The Gospel of Matthew: Introduction, Commentary and Reflections." *The New Interpreter's Bible, vol. VIII*. (Leander Keck, Convener and Senior New Testament Editor). Nashville: Abingdon Press, 1995.

Butterick, David G., *The Mystery and the Passion: A Homiletic Reading of the Gospel Traditions*. Minneapolis: Fortress Press, 1992.

Carroll, John T., "Luke's Portrayal of the Pharisees." *Catholic Biblical Quarterly* 50: 1988, pps. 604–621.

Cartlidge, David R., and David L. Dungan (Eds.), *Documents for the Study of the Gospels*. Minneapolis: Fortress Press, 1994.

Claudel, Paul, "Pilate's Case." *Cross Currents* 36.03 (Fall 1986), 323–331.

Cook, Michael J., "Jesus and the Pharisees—The Problem As It Stands Today." *Journal of Ecumenical Studies* 15:03; 441–460.

Culpepper, R. Alan, "The Gospel of Luke: Introduction, Commentary and Reflections." *The New Interpreter's Bible*, vol. IX. (Leander Keck, Convener and Senior New Testament Editor). Nashville: Abingdon Press, 1995.

Essex, Barbara J., *Bad Boys of the Bible: Exploring Men of Questionable Virtue.* Cleveland: Pilgrim Press, 2002.

————, *Bad Girls of the Bible: Exploring Women of Questionable Virtue.* Cleveland: United Church Press, 1999.

————, *Bread of Life: Lenten Reflections for Individuals and Groups.* Cleveland: United Church Press, 1998.

Felder, Cain Hope (Ed.), *Stony the Road We Trod: African American Biblical Interpretation*. Minneapolis: Fortress Press, 1991.

Felder, Cain Hope, *Troubling Biblical Waters: Race, Class and Family*. Maryknoll, NY: Orbis Books, 1989.

Fitzmyer, Joseph A., "The Acts of the Apostles," *Anchor Bible*. New York: Doubleday, 1998.

Foster, Charles R., *Educating Congregations: The Future of Christian Education*. Nashville: Abingdon, 1994.

Furnish, Dorothy Jean, *Exploring the Bible with Children*. Nashville:

Abingdon, 1975.

————, *Living the Bible with Children*. Nashville: Abingdon, 1979.

Herzog II, William R., *Parables as Subversive Speech: Jesus as Pedagogue of the Oppressed*. Louisville: Westminster/John Knox Press, 1994.

Horsley, R. A., and J. S. Hanson, *Bandits, Prophets and Messiahs: Popular Movements at the Time of Jesus*. New York: Harper & Row, 1984.

Hoyt, Thomas L. Jr., *Proclamation 5: Lent, Interpreting the Lessons of the Church Year, Series B*. Minneapolis: Fortress Press, 1993.

————, *The Year of Jubilee: A Fifty-Two Week Bible Study on the Gospel of Luke*. Printed by Gilliland Printing, Arkansas City, KS, 1999.

Johnson, Luke T. "The New Testament's Anti-Jewish Slander and the Conventions of Ancient Polemic." *Journal of Biblical Literature* 103/3 (1989), 419–441.

Johnson, Spencer, *Who Moved My Cheese?* New York: G. P. Putnam's Sons, 1998.

Jones, Laurie Beth, *Jesus CEO: Using Ancient Wisdom for Visionary Leadership*. New York: Hyperion, 1995.

Kingsbury, Jack Dean (Ed.), *Gospel Interpretation: Narrative-Critical and Social-Scientific Approaches*. Harrisburg, PA: Trinity Press International, 1997.

Klassen, William, *Judas: Betrayer or Friend of Jesus?* Philadelphia: Fortress Press, 1996.

Lampel, David S., "I Never Called Him Lord"—devotional resource: http://dlampel.com.

McGing, Brian C., "Pontius Pilate and the Sources." *Catholic Biblical Quarterly* 53.03(1991) 416–438.

Malina, Bruce J., *The New Testament World: Insights from Cultural Anthropology*. Louisville: Westminster/John Knox Press, 1993.

Myers, Chad, *Binding the Strong Man: A Political Reading of Mark's Story of Jesus*. Maryknoll, NY: Orbis Books, 1997.

"Mysteries of the Bible" video series from A&E Entertainment: "The Execution of Jesus" (1994) and "Herod the Great" (1995).

Newsom, Carol A., and Sharon H. Ringe (Eds.), *The Women's Bible Commentary*. Louisville: Westminster/John Knox Press, 1992.

O'Day, Gail R., "The Gospel of John: Introduction, Commentary and Reflections." *The New Interpreter's Bible, vol. IX.* (Leander Keck, Convener and Senior New Testament Editor). Nashville: Abingdon Press, 1995.

Perkins, Pheme, "The Gospel of Mark: Introduction, Commentary and Reflections." *The New Interpreter's Bible, vol. VIII.* (Leander Keck, Convener and Senior New Testament Editor). Nashville: Abingdon Press, 1995.

Phipps, William E., "Jesus, the Prophetic Pharisee." *Journal of Ecumenical Studies* 14.01, 17–31.

Rush, Charles T., Jr., *Let This Cup Pass From Me: Lenten Reflections for Individuals and Groups.* Cleveland: Pilgrim Press, 2000.

Saldarini, Anthony J., *Pharisees, Scribes and Sadducees in Palestinian Society: A Sociological Approach*. Wilmington, DE: Michael Glazier, 1989.

Sanders, James A., *Canon and Community: A Guide to Canon Criticism*. Philadelphia: Fortress Press, 1984.

Sheen, Fulton J., *Characters of the Passion: Lessons on Faith and Trust*. Liguori, MO: Liguori/Triumph, 1947.

Spears, Larry, *Reflections on Leadership: How Robert K. Greenleaf's Theory of Servant-Leadership Influenced Today's Top Management Thinkers*. New York: John Wiley & Sons, Inc., 1995.

Throckmorton, Jr., Burton H. (Ed.), *Gospel Parallels: A Comparison of the Synoptic Gospels*, Fifth Edition. Nashville: Thomas Nelson Publishers, 1992.

Thurman, Howard, *Jesus and the Disinherited*. Richmond, IN: Friends United Press, 1949.

Thurston, Bonnie Bowman, *Preaching Mark*. Minneapolis: Fortress Press, 2002.

Tolbert, Mary Ann, "The Prodigal Son: An Essay in Literary Criticism from a Psychoanalytic Perspective," *Semeia* 9.01 (1977), 1–40.

Via, Dan Otto Jr., "The Prodigal Son: A Jungian Reading," *Semeia* 9:01 (1977), 21–43.

Watley, William, *From Mess to Miracle and Other Sermons*. Valley Forge, PA: Judson Press, 1989.

Weems, Lovett H., Jr., *Church Leadership: Vision, Team, Culture and Integrity*. Nashville: Abingdon, 1993.

Whitley, Katerina Katsarka, *Seeing for Ourselves: Biblical Women Who Met Jesus*. Harrisburg, PA: Morehouse Publishing, 2001.

Wroe, Ann, *Pontius Pilate: The Biography of an Invented Man*. New York: Random House, 2000.